**New Directions for
Adult and Continuing
Education**

Susan Imel
Jovita M. Ross-Gordon
COEDITORS-IN-CHIEF

MW01089360

The Neuroscience
of Adult Learning

Sandra Johnson
Kathleen Taylor
EDITORS

Number 110 • Summer 2006
Jossey-Bass
San Francisco

THE NEUROSCIENCE OF ADULT LEARNING
Sandra Johnson, Kathleen Taylor (eds.)
New Directions for Adult and Continuing Education, no. 110
Susan Imel, Jovita M. Ross-Gordon, Coeditors-in-Chief

Microfilm copies of issues and articles are available in 16mm and 35mm, as well as microfiche in 105mm, through University Microfilms Inc., 300 North Zeeb Road, Ann Arbor, Michigan 48106-1346.

NEW DIRECTIONS FOR ADULT AND CONTINUING EDUCATION (ISSN 1052-2891, electronic ISSN 1536-0717) is part of The Jossey-Bass Higher and Adult Education Series and is published quarterly by Wiley Subscription Services, Inc., A Wiley Company, at Jossey-Bass, 989 Market Street, San Francisco, California 94103-1741. Periodicals Postage Paid at San Francisco, California, and at additional mailing offices. POSTMASTER: Send address changes to New Directions for Adult and Continuing Education, Jossey-Bass, 989 Market Street, San Francisco, California 94103-1741.

SUBSCRIPTIONS cost $80.00 for individuals and $180.00 for institutions, agencies, and libraries.

ISBN 0-7879-8704-2
ISBN 13: 978-0-7879-8704-6

EDITORIAL CORRESPONDENCE should be sent to the Coeditors-in-Chief, Susan Imel, ERIC/ACVE, 1900 Kenny Road, Columbus, Ohio 43210-1090, e-mail: imel.1@osu.edu; or Jovita M. Ross-Gordon, Southwest Texas State University, EAPS Dept., 601 University Drive, San Marcos, TX 78666.

Cover photograph by Jack Hollingsworth@Photodisc

www.josseybass.com

CONTENTS

Editors' Notes

Most adult educators rely on observation and experience, anecdotal evidence, and philosophical orientation to inform practice. Additional though sometimes conflicting guidance has been available from psychological theories and sociological analysis, which attempt to describe what learning is and how it takes place. Now, however, with the advent of brain imaging we can actually watch the neurophysiology of learning unfold. Not only can we trace the pathways of the brain involved in various learning tasks, but we can also infer which learning environments are most likely to be effective. This volume arises from our desire to make this research more available to colleagues in the field of adult and continuing education.

We have also been deeply affected by our own journeys as adult learners. Both of us went back to college in our middle years to complete long-delayed undergraduate degrees, never imagining that the experience would be life-changing. When we met, years later, we discovered a shared commitment to making this kind of transformative education more widely available for other adult learners. This volume therefore emphasizes ways of teaching and learning that support changes in the brain associated with new perceptions, perspectives, and possibilities.

In the last decade, several studies have been published for nonscientists that explain the inner workings of the brain; some of those authors are represented in this volume. In addition to neurobiological researchers, we have included educators who, in the pursuit of more effective teaching and learning, have contributed to research on how best to change brains. Our volume also benefits from the contributions of clinical psychologists who have established links between improved therapeutic outcomes and current understanding of brain function.

This last observation deserves further clarification. Though they work in different settings (classrooms, therapy offices) and have different intentions (to foster learning, to encourage psychological health), there is notable overlap in what counselors/therapists and educators wish to accomplish. Both groups are concerned with how people think and understand; both also focus on how their client/learners can become more effective in various settings. As is discussed later in this volume, even though adult educators do not act as therapists they need to attend in some degree to the emotional tone of those whom they serve. Similarities and differences between these professional roles are further developed in the chapters that follow.

Although themes of brain function and learning are integrated throughout, the chapters in this volume divide into two sections. The first section

New Directions for Adult and Continuing Education, no. 110, Summer 2006 © 2006 Wiley Periodicals, Inc.
Published online in Wiley InterScience (www.interscience.wiley.com) • DOI: 10.1002/ace.212

1

focuses primarily on brain function; the second emphasizes learning. Chapter One provides an overview of the brain and how it works, with particular attention to implications for educators' practice. James Zull, a biochemist and biologist, describes brain architecture and links brain function to Kolb's learning model, which is familiar to many adult educators. Louis Cozolino, a clinical psychologist, and Susan Sprokay discuss in Chapter Two how the mentor-learner relationship has an impact on the "social brain." They extrapolate principles of adult learning and change drawn from the learning and change known to occur during psychotherapy.

Chapters Three and Four explore the significance of childhood trauma on the brain. Bruce Perry, a psychiatrist, expands on how adult learning may be affected by stress-inducing experiences. He also describes how adult educators can recognize and attenuate these negative effects. On the basis of his practice as a psychiatrist and educator, Colin Ross then examines the educational implications of the potential for brain "self-repair," reorganization of neural networks that can not only alleviate earlier trauma but also enhance current potential.

The next five chapters spotlight educators' practice, using current understanding about brain function as a backdrop. In Chapter Five, Pat Wolfe explores the significance of emotions in learning. She also offers neurophysiological support for constructivist approaches. Barry Sheckley and Sandy Bell, in Chapter Six, detail how the brain uses experience as a basis for learning and consciousness and then describe how educators can use this understanding to inform practice.

In Chapter Seven, Geoffrey Caine and Renate Nummela Caine explore current perspectives on constructivism and "executive functions" of the brain. They also describe strategies for engaging adults in more effective learning. Sandra Johnson, in Chapter Eight, expands on the role of the mentor by examining the mentor-learner relationship through the lenses of cognitive neuroscience and social cognitive neuroscience. Finally, in Chapter Nine Kathleen Taylor links brain function to best practices and constructive-development theory, and describes ways to encourage transformational learning outcomes.

Sandra Johnson
Kathleen Taylor
Editors

New Directions for Adult and Continuing Education • DOI: 10.1002/ace

1

This chapter presents a brain-based model of adult learning and connects the model to practice.

Key Aspects of How the Brain Learns

James E. Zull

Cognitive neuroscience is growing rapidly, and new discoveries appear continuously. Understanding the basic structure of the nervous system and the fundamentals of learning through change in neuron networks can give adult educators much insight. Furthermore, a foundation of basic knowledge is essential in understanding the new and evolving research. This chapter therefore focuses on fundamentals.

How Brains Are Assembled

All nervous systems have the same fundamental "bauplan." There must be sensory elements that respond to outside stimuli, motor elements that generate action, and association elements that link the sensory and the motor, sometimes simply and directly and other times through complex networks that express feedback and iterative functions.

The cortex, a complex layer of cells coating the surface of the brain, is the part of the brain associated most strongly with cognition. The region of the cortex thought to have evolved most recently, the "neocortex," has separate areas for the sensory, association, and motor functions.

Signaling, then, has directionality in the neocortex:

sensory → association → motor

The ultimate value of this arrangement is to allow living organisms to constantly sense a changing environment (sensory) and adapt to it through

NEW DIRECTIONS FOR ADULT AND CONTINUING EDUCATION, no. 110, Summer 2006 © 2006 Wiley Periodicals, Inc.
Published online in Wiley InterScience (www.interscience.wiley.com) • DOI: 10.1002/ace.213

physical movement (motor), either organized and planned movement or more embedded behaviors (association).

In the human brain, the association elements constitute a major part of the neocortex. In fact, there are two large areas of association cortex, each with distinct functions. The first such area is in the back half of the neocortex. It is responsible for association of various aspects of sensory input with one another—for example, shape and color.

These associations are essential for cognitive understanding, but they do not necessarily come quickly. In fact, insight into unsolved problems is enhanced by allowing time for associations to become apparent. This often happens in periods of reflection, or even sleep, when competing sensory and motor activity is at a minimum. With time, our understandings and our associations change and grow.

The second region of association cortex occupies frontal brain regions. It is heavily engaged in conscious association and manipulation of memories and sensory experiences, functions that are necessary for problem solving and creative activity. The most basic aspect of this capability is the planning of actions designed to achieve specific purposes. Thus the frontal association neocortex sends signals to the motor regions, whose neurons are directly connected with the body's muscles, for control of movement (action).

In addition to these four regions of neocortex, there is one other fundamentally important part of the bauplan. This is the ingrowth of neurons that are not part of the sense-associate-act package; their function is to modify the signaling, making some signals more frequent and others less so, still others of longer duration, and so forth. These cells can be thought of as chemical-delivery neurons. They flood cortical neurons with chemicals that then generate the signaling changes. These changes are much slower than the normal signaling, and so the chemicals they deliver are sometimes called slow neurotransmitters. They are ancient, evolutionarily speaking, and their modern-day function is often associated with emotion: adrenaline, dopamine, and serotonin are examples.

Learning and Change in the Brain

The claim that learning is change is more than a metaphor. It is a physical statement. The brain changes physically as we learn. This change has been demonstrated at many levels in many organisms, but here I refer to the most direct study demonstrating change in the human neocortex when learning. In particular, an increase in the density of a small sensory region of neocortex, the region that senses movement, was demonstrated when people learned to juggle. The density of this region decreased when people forgot some of their juggling skills (Draganski and others, 2004): "Use it or lose it!" This and many other experiments have shown that increased signaling by cortical neurons generates the growth of more branches, which increases the density of cellular material and enhances their ability to connect with other neurons—to form more synapses.

These changes occur only in the parts of the brain that are used. They result from repeated firing of the specific neurons engaged in learning experiences, as well as from the presence of emotion chemicals around those neurons.

The Four Pillars. The nature of the change discussed here suggests that learning is powerful and long-lasting in proportion to how many neo-cortical regions are engaged. The more regions of the cortex used, the more change will occur. Thus, learning experiences should be designed to use the four major areas of neocortex (sensory, back-integrative, front-integrative, and motor). This leads to identification of four fundamental pillars of learning: gathering, reflecting, creating, and testing. Experienced adult educators probably recognize in the four pillars the outlines of Kolb's learning cycle (1984), which often begins with a concrete experience of "prehension" (grasping), continues through reflection and abstraction (creating a theory-in-use), and concludes with experimentation.

Gathering Data. Getting information is essential for learning. It is so fundamental that the other pillars are sometimes neglected. One demonstration of this is found in schools or other learning situations where getting information becomes the only goal. This can lead to the assumption that learning is better if courses are crammed with content.

It is important to realize that sensing (that is, gathering data) does not immediately lead to understanding. The data fed into the sensory neocortex are just that: data. A computer analogy has some value here. The data collected by the sensory neocortex are like bits that, by themselves, have no useful meaning. Learning is not equal to data collection.

But it is essential to gather data. Each sensory aspect has its own value. Vision is arguably the most powerful, giving us precise spatial input on objects in the world, and mapping those objects on the neocortex. These maps become the stuff of images that then, along with language, underlie cognition and thought. Auditory data is the core of language, which has both cognitive and emotion content. It also gives us crude mapping information about location. Touch substitutes for vision in that we can use it to create maps of anything within our reach, and it can also provide data about texture, hardness, and so forth. Smell and taste yield qualitative information that is sensed through our emotion system. Sweet, sour, fragrant, and putrid all trigger experiences in our body that we then interpret as feelings. These feelings become part of the sensory data and enrich it, engendering emotional responses.

Reflection. New data flows from the sensory neocortex toward the association regions in the back of the brain. As it flows, bits of data are merged into combinations that begin to produce a larger, more meaningful image. There is a natural hierarchy in these regions of cortex, with the lower ones providing the smaller bits that, together, become the higher ones. It is through

New Directions for Adult and Continuing Education • DOI: 10.1002/ace

these associations that we categorize and label objects and actions and identify the spatial relationships inherent in them. Ultimately the physical relationships are the source of relationships in general. For example, the spatial areas of back-integrative cortex are heavily engaged in estimating the relative value of objects, experiences, and people. These judgments are based on spatial relationships in a metaphoric sense (for example, which is in front?).

Associations occur between memories as well as between elements of sensory data. Thus comprehension depends on the associations between new events and past events. The more past events available to be drawn on, the more powerful the meaning. This can have positive and negative results; adults who have been traumatized by being told they "couldn't learn" or were "bad writers" and so on may have powerful emotional barriers to learning. On the positive side, assignments that encourage students to use negative experiences as a basis for thoughtful reflection and further analysis may help students "reframe" (find new meaning in) those experiences.

Our ability to comprehend new information is also deeply based on assembly of images in the back association cortex. These images are remembered and used as tools in thought. Ultimately, physical images give us the metaphors we use in language. When we understand, we say, "I see."

As mentioned earlier, all this assembly and association of bits of data, memories, and images might be considered the slowest part of learning. It takes time and involves rerunning our data over and over. It takes reflection. Such reflection is often missing in classrooms where "coverage" is the primary goal. Or reflection may be guided almost entirely by the instructor's agenda, leading students to search for "right answers" ("veridical decision making" [Goldberg, 2001]) rather than make meaning (see Taylor's Chapter Nine in this volume).

Creating. The flow of specific meanings or even bits of sensory data from the back association cortex to the front association cortex becomes the basis for conscious thought and planning. It engages what has been called working memory. A small number of relevant individual concepts, facts, or meanings are intentionally inserted into working memory. Determining "relevance" is part of the work. For example, when planning to change a tire, data about tires and cars must be used, not data about horses (or even roads). The chosen information is then manipulated such that a solution to the problem arises. Use of the tire, jack, and car must be organized in sequence. First get the jack, then lift the car, then remove the tire. However, this plan is not just a list of steps; taken as a whole it is a theory, hence an abstraction.

Such plans, theories, and abstractions consist of a combination of images and language. They are the result of intentional associations, selected and manipulated for a purpose. This is the function of the front association cortex, and it represents perhaps the most elevated aspect of learning. It involves intent, recall, feelings, decisions, and judgments. They are all required for development of deep understanding.

New Directions for Adult and Continuing Education • DOI: 10.1002/ace

Testing. Testing our theories is the ultimate step in learning. The testing must be active; it must use the motor brain. Theory must be tested by action in order to complete learning—to discover how our understanding matches reality. Otherwise it remains inert, "merely received into the mind without being utilized, or tested, or thrown into fresh combinations" (Whitehead, 1929, p. 1).

Writing ideas down and talking about them are also forms of active testing. They are physical acts that produce signals from the motor brain, which the body then senses. This changes a mental idea to a physical event; it changes an abstraction once again into a concrete experience, thus continuing the learning cycle.

Emotional Foundation. As was described earlier, all regions of neocortex are enmeshed in networks of other neurons that secrete emotion chemicals. The cell bodies of these neurons are located in the most ancient parts of the brain, the brainstem, but their branches extend up into every region of neocortex. Emotion systems are ancient, but they extend their influence throughout our modern brain.

Emotion is the foundation of learning. The chemicals of emotion act by modifying the strength and contribution of each part of the learning cycle. Their impact is directly on the signaling systems in each affected neuron. For example, in the auditory cortex experimental manipulation of emotion chemicals results in extensive remodeling of responsiveness to high and low pitches (Kilgard and Merzenich, 1998).

Opening the Window of Wisdom

It is clear that there are windows for learning that close somewhat as we become adults. For example, both visual development and language area development in the brain slow down as we age. However, the neurological nature of learning strongly suggests that there is no age of finality for any learning. The promise for the adult is that the window to wisdom may actually begin to open.

This suggestion is based on the idea that learning is a process of continuous modification of what we already know. This constructivist view seems strongly confirmed by neuroscience. Change in synapses occurs whenever neurons are highly active and immersed in emotion chemicals. With experience our networks may become more complex—denser—as illustrated in the juggling research mentioned earlier. This neurological complexity can be a component of wisdom. It is the biological form of knowledge, and the more complex our knowledge is the more we are able to delineate its key elements and separate the wheat from the chaff. This may enhance our ability to make wise choices and plans. I say "may" because wisdom is difficult to define; all definitions go beyond recognizing or experiencing complexity (see Sternberg, 1990). In fact, both neuroscience and philosophical argument suggest the other side of the coin; wisdom is gained when we know what complexity to discard, and when we see basic truths in their most general and least complex form (see Sternberg, 1990, and Zull, in preparation). However, the argument here is that it may be necessary to pass through stages of experience and knowledge that are highly complex before developing the wisdom that helps us know which parts of it can be discarded.

Notes for Educators

As educators of adults, we may wish to revisit our roles and practices as we learn more about the biological basis of learning. Rather than explaining ideas or correcting errors, we may find ourselves more able to trust in learning. This means allowing learners to develop their own representations, theories, and actions instead of attempting to transfer our knowledge to them. Educators cannot give their ideas to adult learners like birthday presents.

What we can give is new experiences. Skillfully designed experiences whose purpose is to generate new ideas and theories in the learner are very powerful (Taylor, Marienau, and Fiddler, 2000). This is especially true when the learner realizes that it is up to her to interpret and explain but finds her existing neural networks inadequate for the task. Adults are most likely to change when a new experience conflicts with their existing theories. Educators can supply such new experiences and raise new questions for the learner to confront (see Taylor in this volume for a discussion of best practices).

When educators' explanations and ideas are framed as new experience, learners need not accept them carte blanche; rather, they are additional sensory data that learners must represent, abstract, and test.

The reader may note that these ideas are not necessarily new and are consistent with many of the concepts of adult learning developed by others (see Knowles, Holten, and Swanson, 2005). However, it is still of great importance to identify where neuroscience is taking us, and to examine how it fits with current concepts and theories of adult learning. Ultimately, our understanding of learning must be consistent with the biological properties of the learning organ. In fact, no matter how widely accepted they may be, all current theories will automatically be reconsidered and revisited as our knowledge about the brain continues to grow.

If this short chapter catalyzes such revisiting, it will achieve its purpose.

References

Draganski, B., Glaser, C., Busch, V., Schuierer, G., Bogdahn, U., and May, A. "Neuroplasticity: Changes in Grey Matter Induced by Training." *Nature,* 2004, 427(22), pp. 311–312.

Goldberg, E. *The Executive Brain: Frontal Lobes and the Civilized Mind.* New York: Oxford University Press, 2001.

Kilgard, M., and Merzenich, M. "Cortical Map Reorganization Enabled by Nucleus Basilis Activity." *Science*, 1998, *279*, 1714–1718.

Knowles, M. S., Holten III, E. F., and Swanson, R. A. *The Adult Learner: The Definitive Classic in Adult Education and Human Resource Development*. Burlington, Mass.: Elsevier, 2005.

Kolb, D. A. *Experiential Learning: Experience as the Source of Learning and Development*. Upper Saddle River, N.J.: Prentice-Hall, 1984.

Sternberg, R. J. *Wisdom: Its Nature, Origins, and Development*. New York: Cambridge University Press, 1990.

Taylor, K., Marienau, C., and Fiddler, M. *Developing Adult Learners: Strategies for Teachers and Trainers*. San Francisco: Jossey-Bass, 2000.

Whitehead, A. N. *The Aims of Education and Other Essays*. New York: Macmillan, 1929.

Zull, J. E. Schools for the Natural Mind: What Ordinary Students, Teachers, Administrators, and Parents Should Demand of Their Schools. In preparation.

JAMES E. ZULL is professor of biology at Case Western Reserve University and founding director emeritus of the University Center of Innovation in Teaching and Education at Case.

2

This chapter is an introduction to how the learning process changes the brain, with special attention to the facilitative role of the adult educator/mentor.

Neuroscience and Adult Learning

Louis Cozolino, Susan Sprokay

Recent work on brain development and learning suggests that the most effective adult educators may be unwitting neuroscientists who use their interpersonal skills to tailor enriched environments that enhance brain development. The brain is a social organ innately designed to learn through shared experiences. Throughout the life span, we all need others who show interest in us, help us feel safe, and encourage our understanding of the world around us. Brains grow best in this context of interactive discovery and through cocreation of stories that shape and support memories of what is being learned. Although many teachers consciously focus on *what* they are teaching, the evolution and structure of the brain suggests that *who they are* may be far more important to their students' learning.

As teachers and therapists ourselves, we are especially interested in how relationships of all kinds initially shape the brain during childhood and reshape the brain later in life. As people move through the stages of life, the brain also passes through various ways of perceiving, organizing, and learning about the world. As a result, the topic of learning (that is, the "what") and the nature of the student-teacher relationship are transformed as the adult student and teacher/mentor join together in a process that changes both of their brains.

Plasticity and Learning

The brain has been shaped by evolution to adapt and readapt to an ever-changing world. The ability to learn is dependent on modification of the brain's chemistry and architecture, in a process called "neural plasticity."

Neural plasticity reflects the ability of neurons to change their structure and relationships to one another in an experience-dependent manner according to environmental demands (Buonomano and Merzenich, 1998; Trojan and Pokorny, 1999). When rats are raised in a complex and challenging environment, their brains increase in the size of the cortex, the length of neurons, the number of synapses, and the level of neurotransmitters and growth hormones (Diamond, Krech, and Rosenzweig, 1964; Guzowski, Setlow, Wagner, and McGaugh, 2001; Ickes and others, 2000; Kempermann, Kuhn, and Gage, 1998; Kolb and Whishaw, 1998). The benefits of stimulating environments are hardly reserved for the young. When adult rats are exposed to training and enriched environments, the effects of earlier nervous system damage and genetically based learning deficits can be ameliorated (Altman, Wallace, Anderson, and Das, 1968; Kolb and Gibb, 1991; Schrott and others, 1992; Schrott, 1997; Schwartz, 1964; Will and others, 1977). Although it is not possible to do such invasive research with humans, there is much evidence to suggest that our brains react in the same manner.

Studies with birds have demonstrated that the ability to learn their "songs" can be enhanced when exposed to live singing birds as opposed to tape recordings of the same songs (Baptista and Petrinovich, 1986). Other birds are actually unable to learn from tape recordings and require positive social interaction and nurturance in order to learn (Eales, 1985). Studies such as these suggest that the proper social relationship may stimulate the neural plasticity required for certain kinds of learning. It is notable that studies with high-risk children and adolescents who eventually have successful lives often mention that one or two people took an interest in them and seemed to care. This is not to be taken lightly; it underscores the fact that, like birds learning their song, people probably engage more effectively in brain-altering learning when they are face-to-face, mind-to-mind, and heart-to-heart.

In a previous book, one of us (Cozolino, 2002) outlined the aspects of successful psychotherapy that enhance neural plasticity. Although psychotherapy is a specific kind of learning, we suggest that the principles of learning are the same in the classroom and across the life span:

- A safe and trusting relationship with an attuned other
- Maintenance of a moderate level of arousal
- Activation of both thinking and feeling
- A language of self-reflection
- Coconstruction of narrative that reflects a positive and optimistic self

These shared elements appear to be necessary for treatment success in a variety of therapeutic approaches; each element finds support in neuroscience research as well. For example, a supportive and caring relationship with another person activates neural circuitry, priming it for neuroplastic processes. A moderate level of arousal—where the learner is attentive and motivated to learn—maximizes the biochemical processes that drive the protein synthesis necessary for modifying neural structures. Though they can be disconnected by fear and anxiety, activation of both affective and cognitive circuits allows executive brain systems to coordinate their activity in support of learning. The ability to reflect on the self plays an important role in integrating multiple processing networks of memory, affect regulation, and organization. Furthermore, the narratives that people construct in dialogue support memory function and serve as a guide for future behavior. Intuitively using a combination of language, empathy, emotion, and behavioral experiments, the most successful teacher/mentors promote neural plasticity and network integration.

The Social Brain

Western science, philosophy, and education share a fundamental conception of the thinker as solitary rather than embedded within a human community. This has led to a focus on technical and abstract exploration of scientific conundra rather than exploration of lived experiences and human interactions. For example, neurobiology and neuroscience have studied the brain through scanners and on the dissection table, but until recently they neglected the fact that it flourishes best within the context of social interaction. However much one may cherish the notion of individuality and the isolated self, humans have evolved as social creatures and are constantly regulating one another's internal biological states.

The notion of the brain as a social organ emerged in neuroscience in the 1970s. Since then, researchers have been exploring and mapping the neural circuits involved in social behavior. Fields such as social neuroscience, interpersonal neurobiology, and affective neuroscience have all emerged to examine how brains interconnect with one another. Although no one module in the brain is dedicated solely to social behavior, there are multiple sensory, motor, cognitive, and emotional processing streams that come together during development to serve social and emotional behavior. It is becoming more evident that through emotional facial expressions, physical contact, and eye gaze—even through pupil dilation and blushing—people are in constant, if often unconscious, two-way communication with those around them. It is in the matrix of this contact that brains are sculpted, balanced, and made healthy. Among the many possible implications of this finding for the adult educational environment is the fact that the attention of a caring, aware mentor may support the plasticity that leads to better, more meaningful learning.

Stress and Learning

In the early part of the twentieth century, psychologists discovered that learning is maximized during a moderate state of arousal. Too little arousal, and students are unmotivated; too much, and they are unable to sit still and attend. The biological basis for this finding has recently been discovered. It turns out that a moderate level of arousal triggers neural plasticity by increasing production of neurotransmitters and neural growth hormones, enhancing neural connections, and cortical reorganization (Cowan and Kandel, 2001; Jablonska, Gierdalski, Kossut, and Skangiel-Kramska, 1999; Myers, Churchill, Muja, and Garraghty, 2000; Pham, Soderstrom, Henriksson, and Mohammed, 1997; Zhu and Waite, 1998).

Stress in the learning environment, negative memories from past learning experiences, or problems in a student's life can also truncate learning ability. One doesn't even have to be conscious of such a stimulus for it to become a conditioned cue for fear (Morris, Öhman, and Dolan, 1998, 1999) that negatively affects learning. By contrast, successful learning may be seen as a "safe emergency"—a state of high attention but without the debilitating anxiety. If the response is a teacher's supportive caring, encouragement, and enthusiasm balanced with an appropriate level of challenge, learning is enhanced through dopamine, serotonin, norepinephrine, and endogenous endorphin production (Kilgard and Merzenich, 1998; Kirkwood and others, 1999; Barad, 2000; Kang and Schuman, 1995; Huang and others, 1999; Tang and others, 1999). In this way, the teacher's interpersonal attunement creates a biological state in the brain that makes it better able to incorporate new information.

Fear is easy to learn and difficult to forget; the brain is biased toward remembering the bad and forgetting the good (Davis, 2002; Vyas and Chattarji, 2004). For many adult learners, the classroom triggers memories of failure and shame that might have once driven them from school. For others, just being in the position of being evaluated triggers stress. Stressors in and out of the classroom can work to inhibit the neuroplastic functions of the brain. With this in mind, one concludes that the most effective approaches to adult learning include some way to address traumatic learning experiences from the past. Although educators are not therapists (and should not try to be), many characteristics of good mentoring echo the literature of effective counseling. Such processes can change the brain by gradually teaching it not to be fearful of the current educational environment.

However, when students examine their emotional learning state their self-identity as poor learners is often revealed and their shame triggered; they may go through a period of feeling vulnerable and angry at their teacher for "outing" them. Even if they successfully break through their negative assumptions and see that they are actually competent and capable, they may go through a period of anger and sadness about the many years they now feel they wasted. Some also experience anger at the people in their past who discouraged and shamed them. Although these issues are not directly addressed in curricula, the most effective teacher/mentors intuitively respond to these personal and internal aspects of education. When doing so, it is helpful if the teacher can identify anger that students may have displaced from the earlier

New Directions for Adult and Continuing Education • DOI: 10.1002/ace

learning situation onto the current one. Through encouragement, not taking anger personally, and finding creative ways for a struggling student to approach difficult material, excellent teachers create emotionally supportive learning experiences that can rebuild the brains of their students.

From a neurobiological perspective, the role of the mentor/educator in adult brain development may be likened to the role of a primary nurturer in a child's brain development. Both offer a safe haven, emotional attunement, and a scaffold to support the learning process. This aspect of the adult educator's task is directly related to the fact that the brain is a social organ and learns best in the context of a trusting relationship. Such a relationship is the developmental "holding environment" (Kegan, 2000) in which adult learning experiences can be optimized.

Thinking and Feeling

Activation of both affective and cognitive circuits allows executive brain systems to reassociate and better regulate them. The orbitofrontal cortex, located just behind the eyes, is a major component of the executive brain system. Damage to its connections with the emotion-producing limbic structures has been shown to affect judgment, insight, and behavior (Mesulam, 1998). In both therapy and mentoring, it is essential to strengthen the orbitofrontal-limbic connections. Teachers who relay factual information and encourage critical thinking are most effective when, acting also as mentors, they help the student acknowledge and integrate intellectual challenges with emotional and physiological experiences. Such an approach helps reduce stress responses; the student is therefore able to calm down and seek appropriate resources. As a result, the neural connections of the orbitofrontal region to the limbic area may literally be expanded. Since the limbic structures are located deep down in the brain, integrating these two areas is called a top-down convergence.

The positive effects caring has on early brain development are echoed in yet another aspect of the adult's learning process. By describing what is happening and reviewing what a child has already experienced, a parent gives meaning to external events and the child's role in them. This kind of dialogue helps the child make sense of his or her own emotional and behavioral responses (Schore, 2001). In this way, the parent helps the child's brain integrate the bodily and emotional functions of the right brain hemisphere with the social and language-oriented functions of the left hemisphere. In times of fear and anxiety, the verbal centers of the left hemisphere tend to shut down, impairing the semantic and narrative aspects of learning that are central to academic success. Decreasing stress as a part of teaching balances hemispheric functioning and activates semantic and narrative processes. A teacher's role in right-left convergence mimics the original parenting dialogue. The role of interpersonal communication as a tool for development is elaborated on in the next section on narratives.

The Narrative of the Learner

The contemporary human brain embodies millions of years of evolutionary adaptation, with old structures being conserved and modified while new structures emerge, expand, and network. The proliferation of specialized networks for motor movement, emotion, thinking, and reasoning created an increasing challenge to keep the brain integrated and functioning as a whole. These interacting networks and the design compromises made in their construction create the potential for great accomplishments and potential chaos. Given that the brain's evolution is intertwined with both increasing social complexity and the emergence of language and symbolic thought, coconstruction of narratives has evolved to serve as an external organizing element of neural coherence and cohesion.

A story well told contains conflict and resolution, gesture and expression, and thought flavored with emotion. All of this is transferred from brain to brain across the social synapse. The convergence of these diverse functions within the narrative provides a nexus of neural network integration among left and right; top and bottom; and sensory, somatic, motor, affective, and cognitive processes in all parts of the brain (Siegel, 1999). Taking a broader view, narratives also serve to integrate the functioning of individuals within groups by teaching specific skills and general values, and creating common blueprints and shared understandings.

Narratives play at least two important roles in adult education: as memory tools and as expression of self-esteem. Because narratives require the participation of multiple memory networks, these stories serve as ways of enhancing memory through linked associations. For example, learning a list of words is far more difficult as a list than it is when a story is constructed containing associations to the elements to be remembered. In addition, the areas of the brain most heavily involved with list learning are also most vulnerable to the effects of aging, medication, and any sort of head trauma. The broad neural base of narratives makes it a more resilient matrix for memory.

In terms of its role in self-esteem, a learner's self-narrative becomes a blueprint for action that can turn into a self-fulfilling prophecy. Adults with traumatic learning histories have incorporated the often unthinking evaluations of parents, teachers, guidance counselors, and other students into their learning narrative. Many adult learners remember hearing comments such as, "Thank God you got the looks, because your sister got all the brains" and "You should sign up for the commercial classes because we need to fill the academic classes with college-bound kids." If such statements are unconsciously or consciously evoked by the learner in a stressful learning situation, they increase stress and decrease success. Under such circumstances, it is especially important to encourage positive and soothing counternarratives.

One strategy is to engage adults in journaling and group discussion that begins with their inner narrative about learning and moves toward development of a new, more capable story. (See also Taylor's Chapter Nine in this volume.) Though there may be some initial anxiety and stress, the connection to others who share their experiences tends to result in the realization that "this is no more difficult than many other challenges I have faced and mastered; just relax, focus, and keep at it." Knowing one is not alone is a powerful antidote to anxiety. In addition, hearing one another's strategies and compensations may give students specific tools for success. Negative learning narratives become a self-fulfilling prophecy in that they increase stress and decrease plasticity. On the other hand, if intellectual challenges are faced with an internal story of an intention to succeed, anxiety is reduced and the neuroplastic processes required for learning are stimulated. For many learners of all ages, trust, dialogue, and healing precede genuine learning.

Wisdom

Wisdom involves integration of thoughts and feelings and blending of experience, perspective, understanding, and compassion. In these areas, adults excel. Adult learners are likely to do better in learning concepts and principles that tie to their experience and allow them to expand existing knowledge. The differences may lie in the areas of the brain that remain plastic later in life. Some adult learners learn better when asked to teach, a position more in line with their place in the life cycle. This peer-learning strategy also embeds learning of information within the social context.

On the basis of professional observation, we note that adult brains have an increasing tendency toward storytelling. This may be due not only to so many brain processes having to converge in storytelling but also to being obliged to transmit information and cultural wisdom to the next generation. It should be considered that adults might learn best through the window of own knowledge and wisdom. For the adult learner, the content of learning and the story of the self may not be separable. The classic narrative drama is a journey from fear to courage, from confusion to clarity, and from crisis to triumph. This may parallel the adult learner's reentry into the classroom. In this way, the self-vision of the learner as a master might have to precede the learning encounter. Adults may need to begin as masters by using their own experience as the basis for new learning. Recognizing and acknowledging the competence, status, and accomplishments of the adult learner activates the scaffolding for new learning. (See Johnson's Chapter Eight in this volume.) This strategy certainly appears to be in alignment with both evolution and brain development.

Current trends in neuroscience are unveiling more evidence that human brains need social interaction to promote neural plasticity. Teacher/mentors who inspire adults to learn may unconsciously embody the neuroscience of education. Their wisdom, enthusiasm, and effectiveness are due in part to an innate grasp of what it takes to support brain development in adults. In any case, understanding the brain's processes further enhances what they may intuitively already know. ·

References

Altman, J., Wallace, R. B., Anderson, W. J., and Das, G. D. "Behaviorally Induced Changes in Length of Cerebrum in Rats." *Developmental Psychobiology,* 1968, *1,* 112–117.

Baptista, L., and Petrinovich, L. "Song Development in the White-Crowned Sparrow: Social Factors and Sex Differences." *Animal Behavior,* 1986, *34,* 1359–1371.

Barad, M. "A Biological Analysis of Transference." Paper presented at UCLA Annual Review of Neuropsychiatry, Indian Wells, Calif., Feb. 2, 2000.

Buonomano, D. V., and Merzenich, M. M. "Cortical Plasticity: From Synapses to Maps." *Annual Review of Neuroscience,* 1998, *21,* 149–186.

Cowan, W. M., and Kandel, E. R. "A Brief History of Synapses and Synaptic Transmission." In W. M. Cowan, T. C. Sudhof, and C. F. Stevens (eds.), *Synapses.* Baltimore: Johns Hopkins Press, 2001.

Cozolino, L. J. *The Neuroscience of Psychotherapy: Building and Rebuilding the Human Brain.* New York: Norton, 2002.

Davis, M. "Role of NMDA Receptors and MAP Kinase in the Amygdala in Extinction of Fear: Clinical Implications for Exposure Therapy." *European Journal of Neuroscience,* 2002, *16,* 395–398.

Diamond, M. C., Krech, D., and Rosenzweig, M. R. "The Effects of Enriched Environment on the Histology of the Rat Cerebral Cortex." *Journal of Comparative Neurology,* 1964, *123,* 111–119.

Eales, L. A. "Song Learning in Zebra Finches: Some Effects of Song Model Availability on What Is Learnt and When." *Animal Behaviour,* 1985, *31,* 231–237.

Guzowski, J. F., Setlow, B., Wagner, E. K., and McGaugh, J. L. "Experience-Dependent Gene Expression in the Rat Hippocampus After Spatial Learning: A Comparison of the Immediate-Early Genes Arc, C-fos, and Zif268." *Journal of Neuroscience,* 2001, *21,* 5089–5098.

Huang, Z. J., Kirkwood, A., Pizzarusso, T., Porciatti, V., Morales, B., Bear, M. F., and others. "BDNF Regulates the Maturation of Inhibition and the Critical Period of Plasticity in Mouse Visual Cortex." *Cell,* 1999, *98,* 739–755.

Ickes, B. R., Pham, T. M., Sanders, L. A., Albeck, D. S., Mohammed, A. H., and Grandholm, A. C. "Long-Term Environmental Enrichment Leads to Regional Increases in Neurotrophin Levels in Rat Brains." *Experimental Neurology,* 2000, *164,* 45–52.

Jablonska, B., Gierdalski, M., Kossut, M., and Skangiel-Kramska, J. "Partial Blocking of NMDA Receptors Reduces Plastic Changes Induced by Short-Lasting Classical Conditioning in the SL Barrel Cortex of Adult Mice." *Cerebral Cortex,* 1999, *9*(3), 222–231.

Kang, H., and Schuman, E. "Long-Lasting Neurotrophin-Induced Enhancement of Synaptic Transmission in the Adult Hippocampus." *Science,* 1995, *267,* 1658–1662.

Kegan, R. "What Form Transforms? A Constructive-Developmental Approach to Transformational Learning." In J. Mezirow and Associates (eds.), *Learning as Transformation.* San Francisco: Jossey-Bass, 2000.

Kempermann, G., Kuhn, H. G., and Gage, F. H. "Experience-Induced Neurogenesis in the Senescent Dentate Gyrus." *Journal of Neuroscience,* 1998, *18,* 3206–3212.

Kilgard, M. P., and Merzenich, M. M. "Cortical Map Reorganization Enabled by Nucleus Basalis Activity." *Science,* 1998, *279,* 1714–1718.

Kirkwood, A., Rozas, C., Kirkwood, J., Perez, F., and Bear, M. F. "Modulation of Long-Term Synaptic Depression in Visual Cortex by Acetylcholine and Norepinephrine." *Journal of Neuroscience,* 1999, *19*(5), 1599–1609.

Kolb, B., and Gibb, R. "Environmental Enrichment and Cortical Injury: Behavioral and Anatomical Consequences of Frontal Cortex Lesions." *Cerebral Cortex*, 1991, *1*, 189–198.

Kolb, B., and Whishaw, I. Q. "Brain Plasticity and Behavior." *Annual Review of Psychology*, 1998, *49*, 43–64.

Mesulam, M. M. "From Sensation to Cognition." *Brain*, 1998, *121*(6), 1013–1052.

Morris, J. S., Öhman, A., and Dolan, R. J. "Conscious and Unconscious Emotional Learning in the Human Amygdala." *Nature*, 1998, *393*, 467–470.

Morris, J. S., Öhman, A., and Dolan, R. J. "A Subcortical Pathway to the Right Amygdala: Mediating 'Unseen' Fear." *Proceedings of the National Academy of Sciences, USA*, 1999, *96*, 1680–1685.

Myers, W. A., Churchill, J. D., Muja, N., and Garraghty, P. E. "Role of NMDA Receptors in Adult Primate Cortical Somatosensory Plasticity." *Journal of Comparative Neurology*, 2000, *418*, 373–382.

Pham, T. M., Soderstrom, S., Henriksson, B. G., and Mohammed, A. H. "Effects of Neonatal Stimulation on Later Cognitive Function and Hippocampal Nerve Growth Factor." *Behavioral Brain Research*, 1997, *86*, 113–120.

Schore, A. N. "Effects of a Secure Attachment on Right Brain Development, Affect Regulation, and Infant Mental Health." *Infant Mental Health Journal*, 2001, 22(1–2), 7–66.

Schrott, L. M. "Effect of Training and Environment on Brain Morphology and Behavior." *Acta Paediatrica Scandanavia*, 1997, 422(Suppl.), 45–47.

Schrott, L. M., Denenberg, V. H., Sherman, G. F., Waters, N. S., Rosen, G. D., and Galaburda, A. M. "Environmental Enrichment, Neocortical Ectopias, and Behavior in the Autoimmune NZB Mouse." *Developmental Brain Research*, 1992, 67(1), 85–93.

Schwartz, S. "Effects of Neonatal Cortical Lesions and Early Environmental Factors on Adult Rat Behavior." *Journal of Comparative Physiological Psychology*, 1964, *52*, 154–156.

Siegel, D. J. *Developing Mind: Toward a Neurobiology of Interpersonal Experience.* New York: Guilford Press, 1999.

Tang, Y. P., Shimizu, E., Dube, G. R., Rampon, C., Kerchner, G. A., Zhuo, M., and others. "Genetic Enhancement of Learning and Memory in Mice." *Nature*, 1999, *401*(6748), 63–69.

Trojan, S., and Pokorny, J. "Theoretical Aspects of Neuroplasticity." *Physiological Research*, 1999, 48(2), 87–97.

Vyas, A., and Chattarji, S. "Modulation of Different States of Anxiety-Like Behavior by Chronic Stress." *Behavioral Neuroscience*, 2004, *118*(6), 1450–1454.

Will, B. E., Rosenzweig, M. R., Bennett, E. B., Herbert, M., and Morimoto, H. "Relatively Brief Environmental Enrichment Aids Recovery of Learning Capacity and Alters Brain Measures After Postweaning Brain Lesions in Rats." *Journal of Comparative Physiological Psychology*, 1977, *91*, 33–50.

Zhu, X. O., and Waite, P.M.E. "Cholinergic Depletion Reduces Plasticity of Barrel Field Cortex." *Cerebral Cortex*, 1998, *8*, 63–72.

LOUIS COZOLINO is a neuroscientist and professor of psychology at Pepperdine University.

SUSAN SPROKAY is a graduate student of psychology at Pepperdine University.

3

Adverse learning experiences in childhood may affect the adult's capacity to learn throughout the lifespan. Suggestions for adult educators are provided.

Fear and Learning: Trauma-Related Factors in the Adult Education Process

Bruce D. Perry

Simply stated, trauma changes the brain. Some of the most persistent changes in the brain involve the capacity to acquire new cognitive information and retrieve stored information—both essential for effective functioning within our current educational system. The result is that, all too often, traumatized children experience the added insult of doing poorly in school, thereby failing within the one setting that might have been safe, predictable, and trauma-free. Even the fortunate children who have not been traumatized outside of school may experience shame and humiliation in the classroom. Too many children therefore grow up hating school, think they are stupid and incapable, and soon give up on themselves and the process of academic learning.

But many grow up to become adult learners who eventually need to return to school. This chapter reviews fundamental issues that may help educators better understand the nearly one-third of the adult population who bring to their classroom a history of abuse, neglect, developmental chaos, or violence that influences their capacity to learn, as well as those who, in response to stress-inducing pedagogical methods, have acquired cumulative educational trauma leading to fear conditioning.

This work was supported in part by grants from the Richard Weekley Family Fund of the Houston Community.

The Brain

Both learning and the trauma response are mediated by, and alter, important neural systems in the human brain. The human brain is complex, comprising hundreds of billions of cells (neurons and glia) organized into thousands of neural networks. The brain mediates hundreds of important functions ranging from heart rate regulation to appetite to motor movement to thinking and creating.

To keep us alive, our brain is designed to sense, process, store, perceive, and act on information from the external and internal worlds. To do this, a brain has hundreds of neural systems, all working in a continuous, dynamic process of modulating, regulating, compensating—increasing or decreasing activity to control the body's physiology. Each of our many complex physiological systems has a rhythm of activity that regulates key functions. For example, if blood sugar falls below a certain level, a set of compensatory physiological actions is activated. If tissue oxygen is low from exertion, or an individual is dehydrated, sleepy, or threatened by a predator, still other sets of regulating activity are turned on to respond to the specific need. For each of these systems, there are "basal" (or homeostatic) patterns of activity within which the majority of environmental challenges can be sustained. When an internal condition (such as dehydration) or an external challenge (such as an unpredictable and unstable employment situation) persists, this is a stress on the system.

Stress is a commonly used term in both lay and professional language. Using a concept more common among biologists, we would say that stress is any challenge or condition that forces our regulating physiological and neurophysiological systems to move outside their normal dynamic activity. In essence, stress occurs when homeostasis is disrupted (Perry and Pollard, 1998). Traumatic stress is an extreme form of stress.

It is well known that adult learners may have experienced maltreatment, shame, and humiliation in childhood, leading to traumatic stress. It is clear, however, that not only do many adult learners have a history of significant trauma, but they are also sensitized to the ordinary demands of schooling. Deadlines, exams, and having to speak in class, for example, will result in moderate activation of the stress response. We know that moderate chronic activation of the stress response systems can also have an impact on key brain areas involved in learning and memory. The end result is that many adult learners are doubly stressed as they return to the classroom setting.

The Response to Threat. The human body and human mind have a set of important, predictable responses to threat. Threat may come from an internal source, such as pain, or external source, such as an assailant. One common reaction to danger or threat has been labeled the fight-or-flight reaction. In the initial stages of this reaction, there is a response called the alarm reaction.

New Directions for Adult and Continuing Education • DOI: 10.1002/ace

As the individual begins to feel threatened, the initial stages of a complex, total-body response begin. The brain orchestrates, directs, and controls this response. If the individual feels more threatened, the brain and body shift further along an arousal continuum in an attempt to ensure appropriate mental and physical responses to the challenges of the threat (see Figure 3.1). The cognitive, emotional, and behavioral functioning of the individual reflect this shift along the continuum. During the traumatic event, all aspects of individual functioning change—feeling, thinking, and behaving. Someone feeling threatened does not spend a lot of time thinking about the future or making an abstract plan for survival. At that moment, feeling, thinking, and behaving are being directed by more "primitive" parts of the brain. A frightened person does not focus on words; he or she attends closely to what appear to be threat-related signals in the environment.

As an individual feels threatened, he or she moves along the arousal continuum from left to right. The further along he or she is on this continuum, the less capable he or she will be of learning or retrieving cognitive content; in essence, fear destroys the capacity to learn. Individuals exhibit differing styles of adaptation to threat. Most use some combination of these two adaptive styles. The adult learner with a history of trauma or with a background of educational failure or humiliation is sensitized and moves along the arousal continuum faster in the face of significantly less challenge or perceived threat.

The person's internal state shifts with the level of perceived threat; as it increases, vigilance may proceed along the arousal continuum to terror. This is characterized by a graded increase in sympathetic nervous system activity, which in turn causes increased heart rate, blood pressure, and respiration, a release of glucose stored in muscle, and increased muscle tone. Changes in the central nervous system cause hypervigilance; the person tunes out all noncritical information. These actions prepare the individual to fight with or run away from the potential threat. The total-body mobilization of the fight-or-flight response is highly adaptive and involves many coordinated and integrated neurophysiological responses across multiple

Figure 3.1. The Arousal Continuum

Hyperarousal Continuum	Rest	Vigilence	Resistance	Defiance	Aggression
Dissociative Continuum	Rest	Avoidance	Compliance	Dissociation	Fainting
Regulating Brain Region	Neocortex Cortex	Cortex Limbic	Limbic Midbrain	Midbrain Brainstem	Brainstem Autonomic
Cognitive Style Internal State	Abstract Calm	Concrete Arousal	Emotional Alarm	Reactive Fear	Reflexive Terror

brain areas. Though it is also the most common and familiar response to threat, it has become increasingly clear that individual responses can vary tremendously (Perry and others, 1995).

For example, whenever physically fighting or fleeing is not possible, people use avoidant and psychological fleeing mechanisms that are dissociative. Dissociation is basically a mental mechanism by which one withdraws attention from the outside world and focuses on the inner world. It may involve a distorted sense of time, a detached feeling of "observing" something happen as if it is unreal, or the sense that one may be watching a movie of one's life. In extreme cases, individuals may withdraw into an elaborate fantasy world where they believe they assume special powers or strengths. Like the alarm response, this "defeat" or dissociative response is graded. The intensity of the dissociation varies with the intensity and duration of the traumatic event. Even when we are not threatened, however, we use dissociative mental mechanisms all the time. Daydreaming is an example of a dissociative event that occurs in many classrooms.

If, during development, the threat response apparatus is persistently stimulated, a commensurate stress response apparatus develops in the central nervous system in response to the constant threat. These stress-response neural systems (and all the functions they mediate) are overactive and hypersensitive. It is highly adaptive for a child growing up in a violent, chaotic environment to be hypersensitive to external stimuli, hypervigilant, and in a persistent stress-response state. These adaptive changes in the brain make a child better suited to sense, perceive, and act on threat in such an environment, but these "survival tactics" ill serve the child when the environment changes (as at school or in peer relationships). Furthermore, the changes in a child's brain related to "use-dependent" alterations in the developing brain can persist to adult life, resulting in a lifetime of anxiety, hypervigilance, and cognitive distortion (Perry, 1998, 1999). The impact of adverse childhood experiences on a host of learning-related functions and outcomes in adult life is therefore devastating (Anda and others, in press).

How Fear Changes Thinking, Feeling, and Behaving. A traumatized person in a state of alarm (for example, thinking about an earlier trauma) is less capable of concentrating, more anxious, and more attentive to nonverbal cues such as tone of voice, body posture, and facial expressions—and may, in fact, misinterpret such cues because of anxiety-induced hypervigilance. This has important implications for understanding how adults who earlier experienced negative learning situations in classrooms might respond in a new learning environment that occurs many years later.

A major mistake one can make with these individuals is to misjudge their internal state. According to Kerka (2002), these adults may have difficulty in risk taking, which could include starting new tasks, responding to questions, or considering an alternative viewpoint. They may have difficulty maintaining self-esteem, and if they feel overwhelmed or inept they may become angry or feel helpless. Some may dissociate, which can mani-

New Directions for Adult and Continuing Education • DOI: 10.1002/ace

fest as going quiet or a glazed expression. More seriously, such students may become avoidant and miss classes. Once we recognize that this is happening, it can be minimized or prevented.

We may think someone is in a state of vigilance and capable of taking our directives when the adult learner is actually in a state of fear. A compound command such as "Take out your book, open to page 52, and write out the key concepts related to the lesson for today" is often processed inaccurately. The learner gets confused and therefore more anxious; this anxiety can then escalate, making the learner even less capable of following directions. If the learner makes a mistake or asks a neighbor to repeat the teacher's clear directives, the teacher can become frustrated and impatient. If this impatience is revealed by word or tone ("OK, I'll say it again") the learner's anxiety escalates still further, possibly leading to a hostile, inappropriate, and immature or dissociative response. This can lead to a cascade of mutual misunderstanding. The teacher is frustrated and the learner comes to dislike the teacher or—worse, still—learning in general and may replicate his or her earlier pattern of disengaging and disinvesting in school and learning.

Baseline State of a Traumatized Learner. Neural systems that are activated change permanently, creating "internal" representations; this is the stuff of memories. The brain makes cognitive memories, emotional memories, motor-vestibular memories, and state memories. The physiological hyperarousal state associated with fear and pervasive threat results in a brain that has created all of these memory types (that is, cognitive, motor, emotional, state) and in doing so has adapted to a world characterized by unpredictability and danger. Such hypervigilant people are in a persisting state of arousal and consequently experience persisting anxiety.

The key to understanding the long-term impact of trauma on an adult learner is to remember that he or she is often, at baseline, in a state of low-level fear. This fear state reflects either hyperarousal or a dissociative adaptation pattern, or a combination of both. The major challenge to the educator working with highly stressed or traumatized adults is to furnish the structure, predictability, and sense of safety that can help them begin to feel safe enough to learn.

A common clinical observation made by teachers is that these individuals appear to be quite bright but at times perform poorly in an academic situation. School has been frustrating and sometimes humiliating for these adults. They come into the adult learning situation with a history of failure, and sometimes with an expectation of further failure.

This context is critically important in understanding why an adult learner with a history of trauma (therefore in a persisting state of arousal) can sit in a classroom and not learn effectively. The capacity to internalize new verbal cognitive information depends on having portions of the frontal and related cortical areas activated, which in turn requires a state of attentive calm. The traumatized adult learner has difficulty reaching this state because different areas of this person's brain are activated and thus different parts of the brain control functioning.

Retrieving Information in a State of Fear. The adult learner in a persisting low-level state of fear retrieves information from the world differently than do adults who feel calm. We are all familiar with test anxiety, but imagine what life would be like if all learning experiences evoked a similar and persisting emotion of anxiety. Even if an adult has successfully stored information in cortical areas, this information is inaccessible while the learner feels so fearful.

In a higher state of arousal, the creative and "mature" problem-solving capabilities mediated by the cortex are not easily accessed. Therefore, when threatened, the individual is likely to act in an "immature" fashion. Regression, a retreat to a less mature style of functioning and behavior, is commonly observed in all of us when we are physically ill, sleep-deprived, hungry, fatigued, or anxious. During the regressive response to the real or perceived threat, less-complex brain areas mediate our behavior. If an adult learner was raised in an environment of persisting threat, he will have an altered baseline such that an internal state of calm is rarely obtained (or only artificially obtained, via alcohol or drug use). In addition, the traumatized individual has a "sensitized" alarm response, overreading verbal and nonverbal cues as threatening. This increased reactivity results in dramatic changes in behavior in the face of seemingly minor provocative cues. A similar, if somewhat attenuated, pattern is often seen with individuals raised in less traumatic homes who were nevertheless subject to shaming and humiliating at home or in classroom experiences.

Safety and Learning

We humans are explorers. We are fascinated by, and drawn to, the unknown—to new things. Curiosity drives us to explore, and when exploration leads to discovery it brings us pleasure. As adults we enjoy finding a new restaurant or new author, or mastering a new skill. Optimal learning depends on this process—a cycle of curiosity, exploration, discovery, practice, and mastery—which leads to pleasure, satisfaction, and the confidence to once again set out and explore. With each success comes more willingness to explore, discover, and learn. The more a learner experiences this cycle of discovery, the more he or she can create a lifelong excitement for, and love of, learning.

The fear or alarm response, however, kills curiosity and inhibits exploration and learning. If people are anxious, uncomfortable, or fearful, they do not learn. If they are unwilling to explore or if they develop anxiety when faced with something new, they place increasing limitations on themselves. How can we prevent this?

The fear response is deeply ingrained in the human brain. When we feel threat of any kind—hunger, thirst, pain, shame, confusion, or information that is too much, too new, or too fast—our body and mind respond in

New Directions for Adult and Continuing Education • DOI: 10.1002/ace

ways designed to keep us safe. Our mind focuses only on the information that is, at that moment, important for responding to the threat. Rather than explore new things, we are disinterested in or even further overwhelmed by novelty. When the learner feels safe, curiosity lives. When we are safe and the world around us is familiar, we crave novelty. Conversely, when the world around us is too new, we crave familiarity. In such situations, we are more easily overwhelmed, distressed, frustrated. Therefore we want familiar, comforting, and safe things.

By accurately attending to the learner's internal state, an effective educator can identify where the learner is on the alarm-arousal continuum. A creative and respectful educator can create safety by making the learning environment more familiar, structured, and predictable. Predictability, in turn, is created by consistent behavior. This implies not rigidity but rather consistency of interaction. The invisible yet powerful web of relationships that effective educators create between themselves and learners, and between and among learners, is crucial to an optimal learning environment (Perry, 2006). In sum, the necessary sense of safety to encourage adult learning comes from consistent, nurturing, and sensitive attention to the learner's state of mind (Daloz, 1999).

References

Anda, R. F., Felitti, R. F., Walker, J., Whitfield, C., Bremner, D. J., Perry, B. D., Dube, S. R., and Giles, W. G. "The Enduring Effects of Childhood Abuse and Related Experiences: A Convergence of Evidence from Neurobiology and Epidemiology." European Archives of Psychiatric and Clinical Neuroscience, in press.

Daloz, L. A. Mentor: Guiding the Journey of Adult Learners. San Francisco: Jossey-Bass, 1999.

Kerka, S. "Trauma and Adult Learning." (Report no. 239.) Columbus, Ohio: Center for Education and Training for Empowerment, 2002. (EDO-CE-02–239)

Perry, B. D. "Anxiety Disorders." In C. E. Coffey and R. A. Brumback (eds.), Textbook of Pediatric Neuropsychiatry. Washington, D.C: American Psychiatric Press, 1998.

Perry, B. D. "The Memories of States: How the Brain Stores and Retrieves Traumatic Experience." In J. M. Goodwin and R. Attias (eds.), Splintered Reflections: Images of the Body In Trauma. New York: Basic Books, 1999.

Perry, B. D. "Applying Principles of Neurodevelopment to Clinical Work with Maltreated and Traumatized Children: The Neurosequential Model of Therapeutics." In N. Boyd Webb (ed.), Working with Traumatized Youth in Child Welfare. New York: Guilford Press, 2006.

Perry, B. D., and Pollard, R. "Homeostasis, Stress, Trauma, and Adaptation: A Neurodevelopmental View of Childhood Trauma." Child and Adolescent Psychiatric Clinics of North America, 1998, 7, 33–51.

Perry, B. D., Pollard, R. A., Blakley, T. L., Baker, W. L., and Vigilante, D. "Childhood Trauma, the Neurobiology of Adaptation and Use-Dependent Development of the Brain: How States Become Traits." Infant Mental Health Journal, 1995, 16(4), 271–291.

BRUCE D. PERRY is a neuroscientist and child and adolescent psychiatrist and serves as senior fellow of the ChildTrauma Academy in Houston, Texas.

New Directions for Adult and Continuing Education • DOI: 10.1002/ace

4

The educational process called psychotherapy offers a model for brain repair through learning.

Brain Self-Repair in Psychotherapy: Implications for Education

Colin A. Ross

This chapter is based on my twenty-five years of clinical experience as a psychotherapist and twenty-five years as an educator. I propose that the kind of brain "repair" possible through therapeutic intervention holds similar promise for certain kinds of educational experience. Recent advances in technology, which make it possible to look inside the brain in ways not heretofore dreamed of, are beginning to confirm these empirical findings.

My goal is to explain the lessons I have learned from psychotherapy about the role of learning in brain repair. Psychotherapy appears to initiate and carry out a program of brain self-repair; in essence, it enables the brain to repair and replace neurons damaged by psychological trauma and biological deficits (Fonagy, 2004). The repair involves creation of countless dendritic connections, which are functional, purposeful, and adaptive. In my view, psychotherapy, education, and brain self-repair are different facets of a single, complex, unified process.

Psychological Trauma and Brain Self-Repair

Twenty-seven years ago, I diagnosed my first case of multiple personality disorder, in 1979 (Ross, 1984), when I was a third-year medical student. For the past twenty-six years, I have been treating adult survivors of severe, chronic childhood trauma with a combination of medication and psychotherapy. During this time, I have had to unlearn much of what I was taught about the relationship between psychiatry and psychotherapy (Ross,

NEW DIRECTIONS FOR ADULT AND CONTINUING EDUCATION, no. 110, Summer 2006 © 2006 Wiley Periodicals, Inc.
Published online in Wiley InterScience (www.interscience.wiley.com) • DOI: 10.1002/ace.216

1994, 1995, 1997, 2000a, 2000b, 2004; Ross and Halpern, in preparation; Ross and Pam, 1995). Psychotherapy was considered similar to handholding and therefore could not affect the brain as drugs do. Only psychiatry could really treat and heal the brain. Psychotherapy, with its creation of a trusting relationship, attention to emotions, and quest for reflection and insight, was deemed ineffective (Arehart-Treichel, 2001).

Twenty-five years ago, when I was in medical school, and later, during my psychiatric residency, it was an undisputed scientific fact that the brain could not repair itself. At the time, we were taught that all it could do in response to injury was create scar tissue; once a neuron was lost, it was gone forever.

The Emergence of a Paradigm Shift

According to Cartesian dualism, body and soul are separate; events in the soul (in Greek, *psyche*) cannot cause events in the body. Cartesian dualism became the foundation of biological reductionism, which in turn is still largely the foundation of biological psychiatry.

From a bioreductionist perspective, mind is an epiphenomenon of the brain, and all causality in serious mental illness runs in one direction: from abnormal genes to abnormal brain function to abnormal mental state. On the basis of this assumption, if the biological machinery were completely understood then all treatment interventions would be at the level of genes and brain biology (Gabbard, 2000).

The reductionism that dominates biological psychiatry does not hold up on scrutiny. Given the view of the brain afforded us by brain imaging, we now know that the psyche, or mind, can change the brain. To put it another way, the reflective process that leads to insight has been shown to affect—and ultimately change—patterns in the brain (Liggan and Kay, 1999).

Virtually all psychiatrists claim adherence to a biopsychosocial model of mental illness, but in my experience this does not accord with operational reality. At the levels of sociology, economics of academia, grant funding, promotions, prestige, and clinical practice, biological psychiatry pays only trivial attention to the psychosocial.

My trauma model theory (Ross, 2000b, 2004) suggests that we are undergoing a paradigm shift concerning the relationship among mind and brain, body, and spirit. Medical advances of the last twenty-five years now demonstrate conclusively that severe psychological stress ("trauma") has certain predictable effects on normal mammalian physiology. As one example, stress causes an elevated level of cortisol in the blood, which in turn affects gating mechanisms in neurons in a part of the brain called the hippocampus. The gates open up and toxic metabolites and molecules enter the hippocampal neurons, causing cell damage and even cell death. The biochemical details of these effects are currently being worked out in basic science labs. We have learned that the brain can in fact repair and even replace damaged or dead neurons. This ability of the brain to repair itself is espe-

New Directions for Adult and Continuing Education • DOI: 10.1002/ace

cially evident in the hippocampus. Selective serotonin reuptake inhibitor antidepressants appear to provide a nonspecific stimulus to neuronal repair in the hippocampus.

According to my trauma model, severe mental illness can result from a biologically normal response to toxic—that is, traumatic—input from the environment but can also be repaired by input from the environment. Brain biology "causes" the mind, in the sense that the chemical, neurological, and anatomical workings of the brain create that which we understand as mind; but the workings of the mind can also modify and—in the sense of creating new, more effective responses to current situations—repair the biological hardware of the brain. Given this reciprocity, psychoanalytical psychotherapy can help the brain, and medication can help the mind. Rather than separate Cartesian spheres, with the mind reduced to an epiphenomenon, we have two spheres interacting through countless feedback loops and mechanisms, just as the genome and the environment interact in a complex bidirectional fashion.

Education—from the root *educare,* to draw out—is a major component of psychotherapy for psychological trauma. Individuals in successful therapy learn reflective skills and develop insight into their inner world. They use autobiographical memory and challenge their old belief systems while restructuring and evolving the "self." It is interesting that transformative learning (Mezirow and Associates, 1990, 1991, 2000) discusses these same techniques, such as challenging assumptions, critical reflection, and restructuring belief systems. According to Daloz (1986, 1999), these techniques need to be implemented within a caring environment.

We now know from brain imaging that these techniques of psychotherapy change and repair the brain. In fact, according to Gabbard (2000), psychotherapy, together with neuroscience, will develop even more specific modes of psychotherapy in order to "target specific sites of brain functioning" (p. 118). Since evidence supports the contention that some therapeutic techniques change and repair the brain, and since these techniques have corollaries in particular approaches to education, it now appears that education of a kind that emulates certain aspects of psychotherapy can repair and modify the biology of the brain (see Perry's Chapter Three in this volume).

Implications of Brain Self-Repair for Education

Experience shows, and we know scientifically, that a child's brain learns to carry out increasingly complex functions as the child matures. The brain of a ten-year-old can carry out conceptual operations such as understanding the conservation of volume, whereas the "same" brain could not do so seven years previously. It therefore follows that the brain is not actually the same; it has grown, developed, and more effectively organized itself. At the level of neurons, dendrites, and synapses, the ten-year-old's brain is different from its configuration seven years earlier.

New Directions for Adult and Continuing Education • DOI: 10.1002/ace

One might compare the root system of a tree that is three years old to the root system of the same tree seven years later. A great deal of structure exists at ten years that did not exist at three. This is easy to see at a macroscopic level with a tree, but there is equally real, concrete, and biologically meaningful growth in the human brain at the microscopic level.

We also know that a child's brain has an amazing degree of plasticity. For instance, it is possible to remove a large portion of a child's brain surgically due to cancer, yet the child can adapt, rewire, and reorganize and be cognitively normal as an adolescent. Until fairly recently, we believed that for all practical purposes brain plasticity falls to zero by early adulthood. Now we are in the process of discovering that this is not true.

These two factors, brain plasticity and self-repair, suggest that education in the broadest sense—as provided by family, peers, the culture—is essential for the brain to grow and organize. The biology is no longer inevitable gene expression driven unidirectionally by the DNA. Rather, genes for brain growth and development are turned on and off by the environment in a complex, rich set of feedback loops. Causality in brain development involves a dance between two partners, DNA and the environment. Learning can therefore either foster healthy, rich brain development or retard it. The same applies to certain types of learning in the educational system.

Certain inputs are actively toxic to the brain, such as childhood physical and sexual abuse, neglect, and family violence. However, plasticity is a general property of the child's brain, and with the proper attention children's brains can be repaired. Given our new understanding of plasticity in the adult's brain and the significant number of adults who come to us with stress-related problems that hinder cognitive functioning, how can we give them reparative attention? On the basis of the changes demonstrated in the therapeutic environment, it appears that an educational system that strives toward similar engagement of higher brain functions might accomplish this task. Educational strategies that engage and develop higher brain functions include narrative, reflection, and provision of a safe or "holding" environment (See Taylor's Chapter Nine in this volume).

Conclusion

My twenty-five years of clinical practice suggest that certain aspects of education—those that correspond to tools used in psychotherapy (creating a trusting environment, narrative, reflection, and insight)—are interventions capable of repairing damaged adult brains. The interesting question then becomes: If a traumatized brain can be repaired through this process, then what about the average brain? Can it, because of greater plasticity and more capacity to connect with the regions that control self-reflection, insight, and critical thinking, become an even more developed brain than was heretofore thought possible? Perhaps educators can collaborate with neuroscientists to explore which aspects of the educational process are most effective in lighting up the portions of the brain that lead to higher-order thinking. Indeed a new initiative, recently funded by the National Science Foundation, appears to be working in this direction. The Center for Cognitive and Educational Neuroscience at Dartmouth College will use a multidisciplinary team that includes researchers from cognitive neuroscience, psychology, and education to explore how the brain learns. The NSF plans on giving more monies to major universities to fund centers for the science of learning (National Science Foundation, 2005).

References

Arehart-Treichel, J. "Evidence Is In: Psychotherapy Changes the Brain." *Psychiatric News,* 2001, *36*(13), 33–36.
Daloz, L. *Effective Teaching and Mentoring.* San Francisco: Jossey-Bass, 1986.
Daloz, L. *Mentor: Guiding the Journey of Adult Learners.* San Francisco: Jossey-Bass, 1999.
Fonagy, P. "Psychotherapy Meets Neuroscience: A More Focused Future for Psychotherapy Research." *Psychiatric Bulletin,* 2004, *28,* 357–359.
Gabbard, G. O. "A Neurobiologically Informed Perspective on Psychotherapy." *British Journal of Psychiatry,* 2000, *177,* 117–122.
Liggan, D. Y., and Kay, J. "Some Neurobiological Aspects of Psychotherapy: A Review." *Journal of Psychotherapy Practice and Research,* 1999, *8,* 103–114.
Mezirow, J., and Associates. *Critical Reflection in Adulthood.* San Francisco: Jossey-Bass, 1990.
Mezirow, J., and Associates. *Transformative Dimensions of Adult Learning.* San Francisco: Jossey-Bass, 1991.
Mezirow, J., and Associates. *Learning as Transformation.* San Francisco: Jossey-Bass, 2000.
National Science Foundation. "National Science Foundation Funds Center at Dartmouth." Press release PR-05-01.http://www.nsf.gov/news/news_summ.jsp?cntn_id=100812. Retrieved Dec. 1, 2005.
Ross, C. A. "Diagnosis of Multiple Personality Disorder During Hypnosis: A Case Report." *International Journal of Clinical and Experimental Hypnosis,* 1984, *32,* 222–235.
Ross, C. A. *The Osiris Complex: Case Studies in Multiple Personality Disorder.* Toronto: University of Toronto Press, 1994.
Ross, C. A. *Satanic Ritual Abuse: Principles of Treatment.* Toronto: University of Toronto Press, 1995.
Ross, C. A. *Dissociative Identity Disorder: Diagnosis, Clinical Features, and Treatment of Multiple Personality* (2nd ed.). New York: Wiley, 1997.
Ross, C. A. *Bluebird: Deliberate Creation of Multiple Personality by Psychiatrists.* Richardson, Tex.: Manitou Communications, 2000a.
Ross, C. A. *The Trauma Model: A Solution to the Problem of Comorbidity in Psychiatry.* Richardson, Tex.: Manitou Communications, 2000b.
Ross, C. A. *Schizophrenia: Innovations in Diagnosis and Treatment.* New York: Haworth Press, 2004.
Ross, C. A., and Halpern, N. *Talking to the Voices: Treatment Techniques for Trauma and Dissociation.* New York: Haworth Press, in preparation.
Ross, C. A., and Pam, A. *Pseudoscience in Biological Psychiatry: Blaming the Body.* New York: Wiley, 1995.

COLIN A. ROSS is president of the Colin A. Ross Institute for Psychological Trauma.

5

The brain, a pattern-finding organ, seeks to create meaning through establishing or refining existing neural networks; this is learning. Emotion affects what is learned and what is retained.

The Role of Meaning and Emotion in Learning

Pat Wolfe

Several decades ago, the traditional measure of learning was behavior. We determined whether individuals had learned something by observing their performance. Learning was explained in terms of stimulus and response; emphasis was on acquisition and manipulation of information. Behavioral objectives were set and instruction was geared toward meeting them. It was assumed that if students concentrated on mastering content, they would retain the information and be able to apply it. But it was also evident that students could do well in a course, judging by the score on a final exam, yet within weeks forget most of what they had "learned." A competing theory of learning, now more widely accepted with regard to higher education, proposed that learning occurred as a result of cognitive structuring and restructuring. Furthermore, students could learn how to learn more effectively in the future. Despite an extensive body of literature, the exact mechanisms of the cognitive approach to learning remained a mystery.

The Neural Basis of Learning

Recent advances in brain imaging techniques now allow us to actually see changes that occur within the brain as learning takes place. We now know that individual cells called neurons are the basic functional unit of the brain and control learning. These billions of cells encode, store, and retrieve information—as well as control all other aspects of human behavior (Squire and Kandel, 2000; see also Zull's Chapter One in this volume).

NEW DIRECTIONS FOR ADULT AND CONTINUING EDUCATION, no. 110, Summer 2006 © 2006 Wiley Periodicals, Inc.
Published online in Wiley InterScience (www.interscience.wiley.com) • DOI: 10.1002/ace.217

When we learn a person's name or how to perform a particular skill, connections between neurons (called synapses) are made, which contain that information. Repeating information or practicing a skill repeatedly strengthens these connections. Scientists are fond of saying, "Neurons that fire together, wire together." But neurons do not work alone; they form networks of connected information. All brains contain the same basic structures, but the networks in each brain are as unique as that person's fingerprints. Though genes likely play some (as yet uncertain) role in brain activity, each brain is sculpted by the individual's experiences.

Memory and Retention. Understanding the brain's learning process sheds new light on what we call memory and helps us understand why our students sometimes have difficulty retaining what we have taught. Though at the cellular level memory is the forming of neural patterns and networks, we do not mean to imply that memorizing is the same thing as learning or understanding. When we talk about memory in this volume, we are focusing on the deeper, more fundamental brain processes necessary to form the lasting neural connections that are the first step in knowing and understanding a concept or other information.

The word *memory* is often used as a noun, as when we refer to our "poor memory." However, memory is not a thing; it is a process of storing and retrieving information. Unlike computers, the brain does not store data in a static fashion. The brain is a dynamic organ that constantly arranges and rearranges its networks to accommodate incoming information. Fortunately, the brain does not, as once thought, store everything it has experienced.

We are constantly being bombarded with all kinds of sensory data—sights, sounds, smells, tastes, and tactile sensations. If we paid conscious attention to all these data, we would be on continuous overload and unable to process any of the information. To deal with this problem, the brain is designed to immediately filter all incoming sensory stimuli and select only those that are relevant at that moment so as to encode them. As the brain synthesizes the data, it makes a decision to drop any information that doesn't fit easily into an existing network. In a sense, we could say the brain is designed to forget. It "forgets," or does not store, information it does not find useful or important.

Unfortunately, much of the information taught in schools fits into this category. The brain does not see fit to store or retain dates of events, definitions of terms it does not understand, or any other data it deems irrelevant. The vast majority of sensory data bombarding our brains are not encoded because the brain does not pay attention to information that, in terms of its existing neural networks, is meaningless (Wolfe, 2002).

Attention. Attention is the first step in this learning process. If the brain ignores the data, they are not encoded and obviously not retained. Physiologically, there are certain types of sensory data that the brain is programmed to attend to, such as loud noises or sudden movements, probably because such attention helped our primitive ancestors stay alive. The brain is also highly responsive to novel stimuli or events (although novelty is not an effective permanent method of gaining students' attention). Novel events become commonplace if they occur regularly; this is called habituation. Starting every class period with a "surprise" quiz soon ceases to be a surprise, and students come to expect and prepare for it.

What then can we use to increase the probability that our students attend to what is pertinent? How do we increase the probability that important data will be stored in rich, permanent networks, to be called on when needed? There are two factors—both of which the educator controls—that have been shown to greatly influence the kind of connection made in the brain that can lead to future recall and greater understanding. They are whether or not the information has meaning and whether or not it has an emotional hook. Adult educators can use this knowledge to the advantage of their learners.

Meaning and the Brain

It is said that the brain is a pattern-seeking organ. It is always scanning the environment to determine if what it is sensing (for example, a particular pattern of light rays or sound waves) is something it has experienced before. To make this decision, the brain searches its existing networks to find a place where the new information "fits." If there is a match, we say the information makes sense, or is meaningful. If there is no match, then the information is, from the brain's perspective, nonsense. In other words, a crucial part of new learning is the brain's reliance on what it already "knows." However, sometimes what the brain thinks it knows is in fact a misconception or misunderstanding; this can effectively derail new learning.

Schneps's study (1989), conducted at Harvard Commencement some years ago, illustrates the powerful hold misconception can have. Dozens of participants were asked to explain why the earth has seasons. Nearly everyone interviewed stated that summer occurs when the earth is closer to the sun and winter occurs when the earth is further from the sun. These incorrect answers were based on the assumption that the earth's orbit is elliptical. That people might have incorrect answers was not necessarily surprising; but that so many had the same wrong answer led Schneps to research the science textbooks that were in use when most of these new graduates would have first studied the solar system. He found that illustrations of the earth's orbit around the sun were consistently drawn from a perspective that, to save space on the page, required an elongated ellipse! Even though the students had no doubt been taught in the primary grades that the earth's orbit is nearly circular and the tilt of the earth's axis causes seasons, and though many of the students interviewed had since successfully completed Harvard's undergraduate astronomy course, the "knowledge" that stayed with them was based on the misleading illustration.

Many inferences can be drawn from this research, including the power of visual images and the capacity of the human mind to take in—but compartmentalize—information that conflicts with existing knowledge. Another inference, however, from constructivist ideas about learning, is that a good place to begin teaching is to first find out what learners already know, on the basis of their previous experiences.

Take, for example, introduction of the concept of median in a statistics course. When students read or hear it, their brains begin searching their neural networks to find a connection. For many, this is their first exposure to the term, and most likely they have no previously stored information to draw on. Unless the instructor intervenes, these learners' primary strategy will be to memorize the definition in the text and hope that it sticks. But, as was said earlier, the brain is not designed to remember what it regards as meaningless information. Test scores are likely to be affected; but more important, learners cannot apply concepts they do not really understand.

Creating Meaning Through Metaphor, Analogy, and Simile. Now let us posit that the statistics instructor understands that adults come to school with well-developed neural networks based on their previous experiences. She realizes that they do, in fact, have knowledge that will help them understand and remember this term. She asks for anyone to suggest an explanation of the word "median," not necessarily one connected to the course. Someone soon suggests the median or middle of a divided highway. The instructor then explains that the statistical median is also a "middle," in this case the middle score of an array. Students can now connect to this not-so-strange-after-all term, and the instructor can use this experience as a springboard to further exploration.

Such approaches are effective in two ways. By drawing on prior experience, adults find a place to connect new knowledge to existing neural patterns. By participating in a current experience—in this case, problem solving rather than "information absorbing"—they create new neural pathways; that is, they construct knowledge. When the time comes to recall and use these concepts, they can draw on more than short-term memory. Using analogies, metaphors, and similes, especially when associated with experiential learning, is a valuable approach for linking new learning to existing knowledge.

Creating Meaning Through Concrete Experience. When learners have little or no previous experiential knowledge to draw on, using current concrete experience is still among the most effective approaches. Problem-based learning, case studies, and other experiential learning approaches have long been designed on that premise (Taylor, Marienau, and Fiddler, 2000). What the new research on learning and the brain now reveals is that when learners are actively experiencing, new neural networks are created in the same way that networks of neurons are created from birth as children begin to experience their world.

Creating Meaning Through Projects and Problem Solving. Problem-solving approaches to learning are effective not only because they are based on experience but also because the brain sees the forest before it sees the trees. Although we are able to examine and understand the parts that make up a whole, our brains work better if they first "get" the context the parts belong to. When curricula and assessment practices focus on discrete parts of the learning challenge, as they all too often do, adults have difficulty remembering—let alone understanding—because they do not see how everything fits together. Even when the author of a given text tries to furnish context for just that reason, it may not gel with the adult student's understanding (that is, existing networks). The brain does not take meaning; it must make meaning. Project-based learning is experiential, cuts across many skill areas and integrates many disciplines, and of necessity starts with a big picture. Once adult learners have engaged at that level, they can more easily and effectively work with the specific problems it presents.

Emotion and the Brain

A second factor that determines whether or not the brain initially pays attention to and retains information is emotion. Emotion is regulated largely by two almond-shaped structures deep within the brain called the amygdala. A major role of the amygdala is to ensure that we react quickly to potentially dangerous or emotion-laden situations—flight or fight, also known as the stress response. During the stress response, adrenaline is released, heart rate increases, blood pressure goes up, senses are more alert, muscles tense, palms become sweaty, blood-clotting elements increase in the bloodstream, and all centers for movement are mobilized. Simultaneously, cortical memory systems retrieve any knowledge relevant to the emergency at hand, taking precedence over other strands of thought (Le Doux, 1996).

One effect of adrenaline is that the memory of the experience is enhanced, which is why nearly everyone remembers where they were and what they were doing when they heard of the attack on the World Trade Center. But adrenaline is also released during mildly emotional and positive events. Therefore, classroom activities designed to engage students' emotional and motivational interest are also quite likely to lead to more vivid memories of whatever grabs their attention. The more intense the arousal, however, the stronger the imprint. It is almost as if the brain has two memory systems, one for ordinary facts and one for those that are emotionally charged.

Adding an Emotional Hook to Learning. Educators can use the power of emotion to affect learning and retention positively. Simulations, role plays, and other experiential activities can be highly engaging. By intensifying the student's emotional state, they may enhance both meaning and memory. Granted, adults are sometimes reticent to participate, at least at first. But if educators also foster a safe environment (see Perry's Chapter Three in this volume), adults are likely to discover the value for their own learning—how much more sense the readings make and how much more easily the content is mastered.

Tackling real-life problems is another way to raise the emotional and motivational stakes. In, for example, a management program, it might be possible for adult students to take on course-relevant problems of local businesses and present their findings to the companies involved. This would likely lead to—literally—a most memorable experience. Similarly, in a course in economics, history, or sociology, students might visit and interview senior citizens about their experiences and memories of the Great Depression. Hearing the information firsthand would create an emotional context that no text could supply.

The Flip Side of Emotion. Someone with no life stress probably would not get out of bed in the morning. Someone with too much stress probably would not either! More is not necessarily better when it comes to the stress response. The ability to experience and talk about our emotions is a singularly wonderful human quality, but it has its downside. The stress response was designed for life in caves, but we do not live there anymore. Unfortunately, the contemporary human brain does not distinguish between actual physical danger and psychological danger; it sets the same physiological chain of events in motion in either case. As was mentioned earlier, during the stress response the rational, problem-solving part of the brain is less efficient. This makes good sense from the perspective of our primitive ancestors: you do not want to spend precious time thinking of all the alternatives when you are faced with a saber-toothed tiger. It is a time to react, not reflect (Sapolsky, 1994).

However, this diminished capacity to think rationally during a perceived threat can be a problem in an educational setting. Even mild stressors lead to initiation of the stress response, which negatively affects the student's ability to perform. Adults perceive many classroom situations as stressful or threatening: simply being in a new course, imagining being laughed at, being called on when not prepared, plus timed testing or a general fear of failure. Emotion is therefore a double-edged sword, with the ability to enhance learning or impede it. Educators need to understand the biological underpinnings of emotion in order to foster an emotionally healthy and exciting learning environment that promotes optimal learning. Our classrooms need to be not only physically safe but psychologically safe as well (see Cozolino and Sprokay's Chapter Two in this volume).

Being psychologically safe means feeling free enough to take risks. Learners cannot make connections if they have been or will be shamed or made to feel stupid for giving a wrong answer or not responding quickly enough. A psychologically safe learning environment is one in which "there is the time, space, and caring" (Daloz, 1999), and enough trust that learners feel they can try out even partly formed ideas.

Making connections is a process, and students may need several false starts before they get to the eureka moment. For most, however, being invited to reflect on and verbalize steps in the process, rather than just coming out with a final answer, helps them become more aware of themselves as learners. Activities designed to encourage thinking through problems, perhaps in small groups, is one effective approach to making new connections.

Conclusion

Much of what has been described here is probably intuitively known to many educators, but now brain scans confirm what are already, in many cases, best practices (see Taylor's Chapter Nine in this volume). Effective, lasting learning is enhanced if adults are given opportunities to make meaning, their existing knowledge is honored, and their psychological needs are respected. In short, adult educators need not become neurophysiologists to effectively use brain-based approaches to teaching and learning.

References

Daloz, L. A. *Mentor*. San Francisco: Jossey-Bass, 1999.

LeDoux, J. *The Emotional Brain*. New York: Simon and Schuster, 1996.

Sapolsky, R. *Why Zebras Don't Get Ulcers*. New York: Freeman, 1994.

Schneps, M. H. "A Private Universe: Misconceptions That Block Learning." (Video.) Santa Monica, Calif.: Pyramid Film and Video, 1989.

Squire, L. R., and Kandel, E. R. *Memory from Mind to Molecules*. New York: Scientific American Library, 2000.

Taylor, K., Marienau, C., and Fiddler, M. *Developing Adult Learners: Strategies for Teachers and Trainers*. San Francisco: Jossey-Bass, 2000.

Wolfe, P. *Brain Matters: Translating Research into Classroom Practice*. Arlington, Va.: Association for Supervision and Curriculum Development, 2002.

PAT WOLFE is an educational consultant whose expertise includes translating current neuroscience and cognitive science into educational practice.

6

This chapter highlights the central role of experience in learning and consciousness; it also outlines experience-based instructional processes that adult educators can use.

Experience, Consciousness, and Learning: Implications for Instruction

Barry G. Sheckley, Sandy Bell

We instructors know that the brain is capable of wondrous marvels. Yet we often get frustrated when we look for examples of these wonders in the student papers we read and the examinations we correct. How can we bring the reality of our students' performance more in line with our expectations?

One way may be to use emerging research on how the brain works. Basically this means designing instruction in accordance with two principles: (1) experience is at the core of consciousness, and (2) consciousness is at the core of cognitive functions.

Experience Is at the Core of Consciousness

At the most elemental level, the human brain accomplishes its remarkable feats by making connections between neurons. A number of these connections are genetically "programmed," such as those that keep the heart beating. Most of the connections form in response to experience when objects in the environment stimulate changes in the state of the body (Damasio, 2003). Simply stated, neurons that fire together wire together (Edelman and Tononi, 2000). The more repetitions we have of a change-of-a-body-state (COBS) experience and the more intense this COBS experience, the more likely the brain is to form a durable, fired-together-wired-together (FTWT) circuit to "remember" the experience (LeDoux, 2002).

For example, when you sip a cup of coffee you are conscious of a COBS as a rapid shift in the temperature of your mouth. If drinking coffee is part

NEW DIRECTIONS FOR ADULT AND CONTINUING EDUCATION, no. 110, Summer 2006 © 2006 Wiley Periodicals, Inc.
Published online in Wiley InterScience (www.interscience.wiley.com) • DOI: 10.1002/ace.218

of your regular routine, the neurons involved would fire together many times. Through repetition, a durable FTWT circuit of the COBS episode would be formed (O'Reilly and Rudy, 2001).

A durable FTWT network can also be formed by an intense COBS experience that is not repeated. What if you grabbed a cup of coffee that was scalding hot and unwittingly took a long gulp? The pain of your mouth burning would lead to an extreme COBS. Even if you never drank coffee again, the magnitude of the neural impulses involved would be sufficient to create a durable FTWT circuit or memory of the event (LeDoux, 2002).

When durable FTWT circuits of a COBS event such as drinking coffee are formed, whether by constant repetition or by an intense COBS event, the brain includes within that circuit not only explicit associations (the restaurant in Belize where you had the best coffee, ever) but also a variety of implicit associations such as nuances in smell, variations in the color of the foam on top of the cup, or even subtleties associated with the brown-eyed person who waited on you. These implicit associations are stored as tacit knowledge. They add another layer to the FTWT neural circuit in the form of a general "sense" or "feel" of a coffee-drinking experience (Reber, 1993).

Experience-based FTWT circuits are also the basis for a wider range of consciousness. In the coffee-drinking example, a slight whiff of coffee brewing at some other time would "fire" a recollection of the earlier FTWT coffee-drinking episodes. In this way you would be consciously aware of the COBS "feeling" of drinking coffee without even actually having any. This conscious awareness can now guide your behavior. Will you drink the coffee? What will you do to avoid another scalding experience? Will you search for another option, a cup of iced tea perhaps?

In sum, COBS experiences are at the core of consciousness. When such events are formed into FTWT circuits, these circuits can expand our range of consciousness and thereby add to the options we have for optimizing behavior. In this way, as discussed in the next section, consciousness is at the core of cognitive processes such as thinking, reasoning, and problem solving.

Consciousness Is at the Core of Thinking and Reasoning

The brain has a remarkable capability to select from interactions occurring among some thirty-two million neurons a subset or "dynamic core" of neural activity (Edelman and Tononi, 2000). With this capability, the brain can enrich awareness of a COBS event that is occurring at the present moment with memories of similar events that occurred in the past (Damasio, 1999).

For example, assume that you have a wealth of experience drinking coffee. When you take a sip of brew tomorrow morning, your conscious experience will occur as a "multidimensional storyline" (O'Reilly and Rudy, 2001). Though consciousness as a unitary phenomenon cannot be separated into constituent parts, for ease of explanation we discuss it here as if it had

New Directions for Adult and Continuing Education • DOI: 10.1002/ace

separate dimensions. One of them would be immediate COBS events—the smell of the coffee, its temperature, the taste of the beverage, and the setting (home or coffee shop)—and your state of mind (late for work, meeting a friend for a chat, or enjoying a vacation, and so on). Second would be the dimension of all past coffee-drinking events: the scalding experience you had with your first cup of coffee, the robust espresso served at the French Bistro, and . . . and . . . and . . . all coffee-drinking experiences stored in your memory. Third would be the dimension that includes all the COBS implicit within your coffee-drinking experiences: the nuances in smell and the subtleties of taste and the social rituals of drinking coffee and . . . and . . . and so on.

Your consciousness also includes the amazing ability of the brain to "extend" consciousness into the future (Damasio, 1999). In this dimension, consciousness involves imagined future scenarios such as possibly being alert at an upcoming meeting, *and* possibly feeling jittery two hours from now, *and* possibly experiencing a let-down when the caffeine wears off. Even though they are virtual, these imagined projections can be experienced "as if" they were actually occurring (Damasio, 1999).

The complexity of the multitextured conscious experience of drinking coffee is a tribute to the brain's capacity for integrating feelings that are based in past, present, and imagined future COBS experiences. If such intricacy is present in a mundane event such as drinking coffee, imagine the multifaceted consciousness of more complex topics.

Think of a group of adult learners, their brains chock full of experiences. Suppose you ask them a political question about the situation in Iraq. Their brains will spark into action as millions of neurons integrate a reservoir of COBS-based FTWT episodes into a multidimensional "consciousness," which they will use to guide the thinking required to respond to your question (Edelman and Tononi, 2000).

Their response is first influenced by consciousness of immediate COBS events. Are they experiencing COBS related to you, their teacher, as a threat? Or perhaps to their discomfort with expressing their feelings in front of others in the class? What about a COBS of surprise because they did not expect this question, or of excitement at the possibility of sharing a passionate belief with others? Their conscious response is also influenced by a lifetime of past COBS events: reactions to newspaper articles they read, their own experiences in the military, attitudes within their family, TV documentaries, and reactions experienced during debates with friends. Their response also includes reactions that have been implicit in their prior experiences, such as a COBS in response to a sense of foreboding about another attack; or a COBS based on unconscious associations between Iraq and the Vietnam War. Their conscious response is also influenced by imagined future scenarios as if they were happening in the moment. They unconsciously imagine COBS reactions as if they were called to military duty; their nephew serving in Baghdad was killed; terrorists attacked during an upcoming trip to New York City; their answer alienated them from others in the class; their answer caused you to lower a grade.

In similar fashion, if you ask them to analyze a case study of business ethics from recent newspaper headlines, these responses are again guided by a multidimensional consciousness. In addition to the possibility that adult learners may be struggling with tired COBS from a long day of work, their various workplace experiences influence their responses. Perhaps they resonate to the case with an enthusiastic COBS because they imagine themselves using information from the discussion to solve a similar situation on their job. They may also experience a wary COBS, from prior experience with case studies and a tacit sense that there is more to this one than meets the eye.

Whatever the topic—the situation in Iraq, corporate misbehavior, or even drinking a cup of coffee—the cognitive processes of thinking, reasoning, and decision making are grounded in the immediate COBS experience of the moment. In turn, this conscious experience is integrated into a cohesive storyline based in COBS episodes that occurred in the past, COBS episodes that they imagine could occur in the future, as well as a tacit sense or feel of the situation grounded in COBS implicit in their prior experiences. Individuals with few COBS episodes related to the notions of war, management, or drinking coffee have a relatively narrow consciousness of these topics because they have fewer COBS feelings to draw on. In jargon, they are "clueless." Individuals with a broad range of COBS experiences, however, have the potential for constructing a conscious experience that has greater depth and breadth, because their lifelong storyline related to these concepts is more extensive.

Instructional Strategies and Consciousness

Instructors who understand that experience-based COBS episodes are at the core of consciousness, that consciousness is multidimensional, and that consciousness in its various forms is at the core of many cognitive processes can plan instructional activities accordingly. In the next sections, we outline a few strategies we have found helpful in orchestrating an experience-based instructional process that adds depth and breadth to the consciousness that guides learners' cognitive processes.

Strategy One: Begin with the Baseline of Prior Experience. As outlined in the prior sections, students are not a blank slate when they enter a learning situation. For this reason, instructors—as a first step in enhancing learning—can focus on the consciousness students bring to the learning event. Starting at any other point "will be a recipe for wasted effort, unnecessary costs, and frustration" (Keeton, Sheckley, and Griggs, 2002, p. 49). Instructors can ask students about their immediate reactions, prior experiences, and future situations. Such queries may occur as a class discussion, an interview, a portfolio, or a short essay.

The responses can help instructors refine and adapt their strategies. They can use this information to alleviate situations that might deter learning, such as a student's conscious worries about doing math. Instructors can create situations to enhance learning, such as offering independent study

New Directions for Adult and Continuing Education • DOI: 10.1002/ace

options that build on conscious excitement about solving a problem or attaining a personal goal.

Also, since learners will judge as valuable information that is linked to the feelings based in their life-sustaining COBS history, instructors may use learners' prior experiences as Velcro strips onto which new concepts or ideas can adhere. Many approaches are possible (Keeton, Sheckley, and Griggs, 2002). Instructors can encourage learners to reflect on their prior experiences and identify the assumptions about an issue that are based on these experiences. Instructors can then ask students to build from these assumptions by exploring alternative perspectives, contrasting their assumptions with other explanations, or checking the validity of inferences they have made. Instructors can also form students into groups where they compare their experience-based perspectives with those of other students and then debate differences of opinion.

Information on learners' prior COBS-based consciousness may also give instructors clues regarding the misconceptions learners have about the topic being addressed (see Wolfe's Chapter Five in this volume, for an example of how misconceptions can arise and persist). With this revelation, instructors can focus on helping learners reconstruct notions that may interfere with learning new information. By addressing such misunderstandings, instructors can help learners expand the complexity and precision of thought they use to comprehend a situation or plan a course of action.

Instructors can also help learners integrate their prior experiences into a cohesive, multidimensional consciousness of their past history. This integrated storyline can in turn enhance students' problem-solving capabilities. For example, a research study we conducted found that in the task of solving complex problems students who integrated their lifetime history of COBS-based experiences into an organized storyline by compiling portfolios of their prior learning outperformed students who did not construct such integrated storylines of their learning (LeGrow, Sheckley and Kehrhahn, 2002).

Strategy Two: Extend Learners' Consciousness. Learners can usually make connections between current and prior COBS experiences: "This is what I feel right now; this is how it relates to episodes in my past life." In contrast, learners often encounter difficulties when trying to extend their experience-based consciousness to make sense of situations that are not analogous to their past history (Gentner and Markham, 1997; Voss and Post, 1988). Instructors can help students overcome this difficulty.

Immanuel Kant, in his *Critique of Pure Reason,* stated that concepts (ideas) without percepts (experience-based consciousness) are empty; percepts without concepts are blind (Kant, 1897). In other words, personal consciousness based only in COBS episodes is "blind" in that the extension of consciousness to include situations outside the realm of experience may not be apparent to some learners. New ideas, concepts, and perspectives can help these learners "see" their experiential consciousness in a broader perspective and allow them to generalize and apply their consciousness in a wider range of situations. But, as discussed previously in strategy one, without a connection to their experience-based consciousness, learners will experience any new idea in and of itself as "empty."

A crucial instructional step in enhancing learners' ability to extend consciousness to novel situations involves assisting them to learn new concepts that open their eyes and literally remove the blinders of their prior experience. A companion step is to fill the emptiness of these new ideas, concepts, or theories with "life" by linking this new information to learners' COBS-based consciousness, perhaps by helping them reflect on their prior experiences. By making connections between a new concept and elements of their personal experience-based consciousness, learners can bring both life and meaning to new ideas.

For example, students who enroll in our doctoral program in adult learning have an already multidimensional consciousness about how adults learn. For starters, they have their own COBS feelings about being adult learners. They also have a host of COBS experiences as trainers, curriculum developers, and designers of instructional programs for adults. When we, as faculty, present them with a situation in which they have to think through how to help adults learn best, they use these multiple dimensions of their personal consciousness. However, many times this consciousness blinds them to new possibilities. Our job as instructors, then, is to expand the layers of their consciousness—remove areas of blindness—so their consciousness of adult learning has a broader and richer texture. In doing so, we also help learners make connections between these new perspectives and their prior experiences. Without this connection, the new idea would not have life.

For example, we continuously invite learners to reconsider their multidimensional consciousness of adult learning by introducing them to new experiences (interviews with adult learners on how they learned to be proficient in their job), new ideas (research indicating that very little information learned in a classroom setting is actually used in practice), new perspectives (the role of learning in the survival of African villages). As we introduce each new experience, idea, or perspective, we assist learners to integrate them into their conscious experience of adult learning through concept mapping ("CMap Tools," 2005).

From research showing that experts (in contrast to novices) use well-structured conceptual models to extend their consciousness (Wiley, 1998), we work to help learners construct well-structured conceptual models similar to those that experts use. Concept mapping is an invaluable tool in this process. Typically at an initial class meeting, as we outline the ideas and topics covered in the course we also indicate that participants in the course will construct their own conceptual model of how adults learn. We stress that this representation will be based on the multiple dimensions of their consciousness. Immediate COBS experiences they have in the course as adult learners will come into play. Their past experiences working with adult learners in their professional work will also have an influence. To this mix they will add ideas and theories covered throughout the semester.

New Directions for Adult and Continuing Education • DOI: 10.1002/ace

During each class meeting we discuss the fit: How does this reading fit with your personal consciousness of adult learners? Does the reading for this week match your prior experiences? Does it conflict in any way? How would you integrate your experience with these readings? From the discussion, students build a concept map—a representation that evolves over the course of the semester—as seen in Figure 6.1.

Figure 6.1 is the final map produced by a student who worked through the concept-mapping process in one of our courses. In his end-of-course interview, he indicated that the ideas of individual characteristics and the role of the environment that are included in the map were based on COBS experiences he had prior to the course. He also indicated that the new ideas he encountered in the course (deliberate practice, metacognition, self-regulation, and others) supplemented his prior experiences, extended his conscious awareness of adult learners, and improved his effectiveness as a professional educator.

Strategy Three: Enrich Consciousness. Knowing that COBS experiences are the basis for establishing FTWT episodes that enrich consciousness, instructors may consider activities that have a high possibility of prompting COBS episodes (see Taylor, Marienau, and Fiddler, 2000). To this end, instructors might incorporate into their lessons provocative events such as real-life

Figure 6.1. Concept Map on Adult Learning

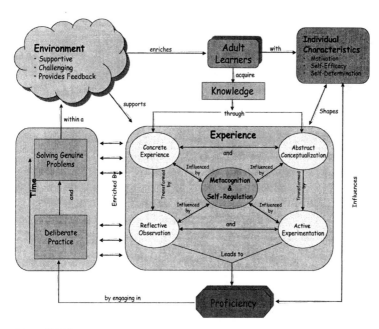

Source: Massa (2001).

problems adults are grappling with at work, debate on topics such as the constitutionality of *Roe* v. *Wade,* activities that link historical events such as the Battle of Hastings in 1066 with their lives today, research projects such as conducting an opinion poll about the invasion of Iraq, or simulations such as managing a mock stock portfolio. The nature of the instructional activity is critical. Without a COBS experience that is sufficient to form FTWT circuits, no "memory" of the episode is registered; no "learning" occurs.

Instructors can also enrich learners' consciousness with layers of tacit knowledge. When learners are involved in complex activities such as making a sales call, debugging a computer program, reviewing the intricacies of a historical event, or writing an article for publication, they learn "implicitly" the complex patterns literally "tangled" within these situations (Edelman and Tononi, 2000). This implicit learning occurs without direct instruction (Broadbent, Fitzgerald, and Broadbent, 1986). The tacit or "preconscious" knowledge so learned appears to augment an FTWT network with an almost intuitive sense or feel of how to work most successfully in complex situations (Reber, 1993). Instructors interested in enhancing their students' tacit knowledge can do so by involving the learners directly in complex situations with the understanding (or even faith) that the basal ganglia system within a learner's brain will "learn" implicitly the complex patterns involved in the situation.

Instructors who enhance learning by orchestrating a range of activities that prompt COBS experiences do a valuable service for these students. The broader the dimensions of COBS feelings these learners have, the greater is the depth and breadth of the resources they can call on when thinking, reasoning, and making decisions.

Conclusion

Throughout this chapter we argue that experiences are the building blocks of consciousness and that in turn this multidimensional consciousness guides cognitive processes. Though sitting in a classroom listening to a lecture might result in a COBS that expands consciousness, from the perspective of research on how the brain works such lecture-discussion activities may be among the least effective ways to enhance learning. Far more effective are instructional strategies that build on prior experiences, engage learners in activities that enable them to extend their consciousness to novel situations beyond the realm of their prior experience, add layers of tacit knowledge, and enrich their consciousness with a range of experiences.

Instead of always bringing learners to classrooms, faculty members could work directly with learners in the work and life settings where they experience the COBS events that are at the core of their consciousness. We tested the viability of several strategies outlined in this chapter by working onsite with agents in a call center of a financial firm. An in-depth evaluation using both qualitative and quantitative data showed that, as a result of the experience-based program, participants improved not only in performance but also in the complexity of their thought, their tolerance for ambiguity, and exercise of autonomy that generalized beyond the job setting to include an array of life and career choices. The outcomes demonstrated, first, that learning was enhanced when experiences encountered in the job setting were the basis for student learning and, second, that the gains achieved in cognitive development and metacognition rivaled those achieved in traditional courses we teach on campus (Sheckley and Bell, 2005).

As ongoing brain research increases our understanding of how experience enriches consciousness, our hope is that this knowledge will be used to guide reform and innovation in higher education. We imagine a time when instructors teach adults using processes that more closely match how they actually learn.

References

Broadbent, D. E., Fitzgerald, P., and Broadbent, M.H.P. "Implicit and Explicit Knowledge in the Control of Complex Systems." *British Journal of Psychology*, 1986, *77*, 33–50.

"CMap Tools: Knowledge Modeling Kit." 2005. http://cmap.ihmc.us/; retrieved Jan. 20, 2006.

Damasio, A. *The Feeling of What Happens: Body and Emotion in the Making of Consciousness.* Orlando: Harcourt Brace, 1999.

Damasio, A. *Looking for Spinoza: Joy, Sorrow, and the Feeling Brain.* Orlando: Harcourt Brace, 2003.

Edelman, G. M., and Tononi, G. *A Universe of Consciousness: How Matter Becomes Imagination.* New York: Basic Books, 2000.

Gentner, D., and Markham, A. B. "Structure Mapping in Analogy and Similarity." *American Psychologist,* 1997, *52*(1), 45–56.

Kant, I. *Critique of Pure Reason* (J.M.D. Meiklejohn, trans.). London: George Bell, 1897.

Keeton, M. T., Sheckley, B. G., and Griggs, J. *Effectiveness and Efficiency in Higher Education for Adults: A Guide for Fostering Learning.* Dubuque: Iowa: Kendall/Hunt, 2002.

LeDoux, J. *The Synaptic Self.* New York: Simon and Schuster, 2002.

LeGrow, M., Sheckley, B. G., and Kehrhahn, M. T. "Comparison of Problem-Solving Performance Between Adults Receiving Credit via Assessment of Prior Learning and Adults Completing Classroom Courses." *Journal of Continuing and Higher Education,* 2002, *50*(3), 1–13.

Massa, N. *Concept Map on Adult Learning: Department of Educational Leadership.* Storrs: University of Connecticut, 2001.

O'Reilly, R. C., and Rudy, J. W. "Conjunctive Representations of Learning and Memory: Principles of Cortical and Hippocampal Function." *Psychological Review,* 2001, *108*(2), 311–345.

Reber, A. S. *Implicit Learning and Tacit Knowledge: An Essay on the Cognitive Unconscious* (vol. 19, Oxford Psychology Series). New York: Oxford University Press, 1993.

Sheckley, B. G., and Bell, A. "Increasing Call Agents' Proficiency: A Successful Corporate-University Partnership." In B. Sugrue, S. Carliner, and R. Cote (eds.), *Proceedings of the First ASTD Research-to-Practice Conference-within-a-Conference.* Alexandria, Va.: ASTD Press, 2005.

Taylor, K., Marienau, C., and Fiddler, M. *Developing Adult Learners: Strategies for Teachers and Trainers.* San Francisco: Jossey-Bass, 2000.

Voss, J. F., and Post, T. A. "On the Solving of Ill-Structured Problems." In M.T.H. Chi, R. Glaser, and M. J. Farr (eds.), *The Nature of Expertise.* Mahwah, N.J.: Erlbaum, 1988.

Wiley, J. "Expertise as Mental Set: The Effects of Domain Knowledge in Creative Problem Solving." *Memory and Cognition,* 1998, 26(4), 716–730.

BARRY G. SHECKLEY is Ray Neag Professor of Adult Learning and department head, Department of Educational Leadership, Neag School of Education, University of Connecticut.

SANDY BELL is assistant professor and section head of the adult learning program in the Department of Educational Leadership, Neag School of Education, University of Connecticut.

7

Research on the executive functions of the brain supports a constructivist, experiential approach to teaching and learning.

Meaningful Learning and the Executive Functions of the Brain

Geoffrey Caine, Renate Nummela Caine

The issue we address here is the link between effective decision making and meaningful learning. We define meaningful learning in terms of the doctrine of constructivism, and we look at decision making in terms of what neuroscientists call the executive functions. Of course, neuroscience is not needed to establish the existence or importance of decision making. However, by examining the issue through the lens of the executive functions, we gain some insight into the mechanisms at work and, more usefully, gain real insight into what happens when the capacity to make important decisions is compromised or sabotaged.

The Meaning of "Learning"

Several overlapping terms and processes are associated with learning: memorization, gaining understanding, having an insight, behavioral change, skill development, maturation, and others. Lack of space precludes us from exploring most of these differences here, so we concentrate on the making of meaning, or in simpler terms, learning as making sense of things.

One way in which this aspect of learning has long been framed is through the doctrine of constructivism, a "view of learning in which learners use their own experiences to construct understandings that make sense to them, rather than having understanding delivered to them in already organized form" (Kauchak and Eggen, 1998, p. 184). Constructivism has had a fairly long and contentious history and is the basis for a variety of concerns. For instance, there is vigorous disagreement about whether it actu-

NEW DIRECTIONS FOR ADULT AND CONTINUING EDUCATION, no. 110, Summer 2006 © 2006 Wiley Periodicals, Inc.
Published online in Wiley InterScience (www.interscience.wiley.com) • DOI: 10.1002/ace.219

ally describes what human learners do (Bennett, Finn, and Cribb, 2000), and constructivists themselves disagree about whether the construction of meaning is essentially an individual or a social process.

We have argued, on the basis of research from both cognitive psychology and the neurosciences, that in order to adequately understand any concept, or acquire any mastery of a skill or domain, a person has to make sense of things for himself or herself, irrespective of how much others know and how much a coach, mentor, or teacher tries to help. We have also argued that although there is an indispensable social aspect to the construction of meaning, there is also an irreducible individual element (Caine and Caine, 1994, 2001; Caine, Caine, McClintic, and Klimek, 2005).

One consequence of a new construction of meaning is a shift in perception, in how a person sees the world and himself or herself in it. We have suggested that "people who 'get it' have acquired a new way of looking at the world. That means that they can see the problems that they could not see before; they can grasp the needs of the situation. Those who have not made this perceptual shift literally cannot read contexts in a fresh way. Their training does not transfer because they were not equipped with the perceptual lenses that are needed to operate in new environments" (Caine and Caine, 2001, p. 69). Thus Goethe spoke of "new organs of cognition" (Zajonc, 1993).

For the shift in perception to occur as people make sense of things, they have to have an adequate amount of relevant experience. People learn from experience in a way that is simply not possible from instruction or information delivery alone (see also Sheckley and Bell's Chapter Six in this volume). The reason is that a perceptual shift requires more than intellectual understanding. The shift needs to be embodied because the psychophysiological system as a whole is what gets it (Caine, 2004). The embodiment of meaning is only slowly becoming recognized in the academic world (see, for example, Damasio, 1999; Varella, Thompson, and Rosch, 1995; Lakoff and Johnson, 1999). However, the essence of embodied meaning is found throughout everyday life, whenever one speaks of getting a feel for things (Caine and Caine, 2001).

Experience is important because it is only through a substantial range of relevant experience that the entire system can be adequately engaged. Thus learners need to navigate through a world of experience in which curriculum is embedded so that meaning is acquired as a result of seeing how concepts and skills play themselves out in context. This process has been addressed through constructs such as situated cognition (Lave and others, 1991) and cognitive coaching (Collins, Brown, and Holum, 1991).

It should be noted that the word *experience* has both a narrow and a broad meaning. For example, reading a book and listening to someone talk about a topic to be learned are also experience. However, meaningful learning has to do with the extent to which one is fully engaged in reading and listening. An engaged reader—one who brings his or her thoughts and questions to a book—reads differently from someone who simply surfs the overt meanings of the words. More of the body, brain, and mind of the engaged reader are participating.

Yet even here, more than reading is needed to make adequate sense of what is being read. At some stage, there is a need for physical and sensory participation or recall of sensory and physical events to which the reading can be connected if full meaning is to emerge. So, for instance, notwith-standing how good a book is on the art of supervision and management, the student must attentively participate in the act of supervising or being super-vised, or be able to recall and think about such events from the past, in order to fully get the essence of supervision.

Actor-Centered Adaptive Decision Making

It is not enough, however, for a person to simply have experience. An essen-tial aspect of learning from experience is making relevant decisions. In everyday life, people perceive and interpret a situation, and then to a lesser or greater extent they decide on an appropriate response, what to pay fur-ther attention to, how to deal with feedback, what to pursue, and so on. They are engaged in what Elkhonon Goldberg (2001) calls actor-centered adaptive decision making (ACADM) or "executive leadership decisions." Thus Goldberg writes that "[most] executive leadership decisions are pri-ority based, are made in ambiguous environments, and are adaptive, rather than veridical, in nature. The cognitive processes involved in resolving ambiguous situations through priorities are very different from those involved in solving strictly deterministic situations" (p. 79).

Whenever there is a clear right or wrong answer, a decision is veridi-cal. Any action that is based on a "recipe," such as filling in specific blank spaces on a form or recalling and reciting the characters in a novel, involves veridical decisions. On the other hand, any problem or situation that requires interpretation of what is happening and a choice of action involves ACADM. Real-life examples abound: driving in heavy traffic, deciding what to do with a difficult customer, and making decisions in the context of a dis-aster such as that caused by the force of nature—a hurricane, a tsunami, an earthquake. In learning environments, ill-structured problems are those that require nonveridical discrimination and response and are far more effective in teaching the skills of analysis and critical thinking.

Actor- (or learner-) centered adaptive decision making is the key to constructivist learning. The learner finds himself or herself in an ambigu-ous situation that calls for decisions to be made involving some aspect of the field of study. This applies as much to someone in a laboratory as at the point of sale or performing an audit. It is in the making of those decisions and in dealing with feedback that people come to make sense of things and acquire useful knowledge. Learner-centered adaptive decision making (LCADM) operates on at least two levels (Collins, Brown, and Holum, 1991). As a person masters a domain, there are decisions based on strategies for solving problems within the domain; and there are control strategies and processes. These involve processes addressed in such other terms as applied metacognition (Perfect and Schwartz, 2002), self-efficacy (Bandura, 2000), and self-regulation (Schwartz and Shapiro, 1976).

Imagine, for instance, that a person wants to master the art of preparing income tax returns. At one level, there is the need to grasp and organize the particulars supplied by a client with the tax code and procedures in mind. At another level is the need to be able to pace and monitor one's workload (especially as April 15 approaches) and to be able to deal with irritations, miscommunication, troublesome clients, and the need to be able to research specific questions as and when they arrive. With slight variations, essentially the same process obtains when an adult learner is engaged with an experience-based, constructivist curriculum.

Effective decision making along the lines just described requires integration of many aspects of human functioning, ranging from content knowledge through mastery of one's own emotions to the many aspects of life (or learning) management. Neuroscientists have begun to investigate these capacities and how they are integrated under the guise of what they call the executive functions of the human brain.

The Executive Functions

The executive functions refer to a number of functions centered largely in the frontal and prefrontal cortex of the brain (located behind the forehead). This area is associated with coordination and synthesis of emotions, thinking, memory, and body or physical movement. Thus the executive functions play a crucial role in integrating many processes, and therefore in the problem-solving and control processes referred to earlier.

Goldberg (2001) compares the executive functions to the role that an orchestra conductor plays. The conductor does not play an instrument or in any way do what the members of the orchestra are doing but, rather, is in charge of how the entire piece of music comes together—determining how loud the oboe plays and when the violins need to come to the foreground, and influencing how the soloists are integrated. All of this is happening as the conductor moderates the volume, pace, and rhythm of the music.

What the conductor does for the orchestra is somewhat analogous to what the group of functions referred to as the executive functions do in the brain. They combine elements of affect, self-regulation, working memory, and inhibition. Thus Boone (1999) suggests that the term *executive functions* refers to abilities involved in volition, planning, purposeful action, and effective performance. Denkla (1999) also suggests that the executive functions are central to higher-order cortical operations and have strong overlap with attention and memory.

At the heart of the executive functions is "the ability to maintain an appropriate problem-solving set for attainment of future goal" (Pennington,

Vennetto, McAleer, and Roberts, 1999, p. 586), which is also called working memory. Working memory refers to the ability to maintain plans and program in mind or "online" until necessary, in order to complete a specific action or plan. Working memory also allows an individual to override an automatic response and shift problem-solving strategies to an alternate solution (also referred to as flexibility).

Although the ambit of the executive functions is still vague, they can clearly be seen at the heart of decision making and the control strategies and processes we have described. A direct and practical corollary for educators is, as was already suggested, that the best way to help students develop and engage their executive functions is to adopt a constructivist approach to teaching and learning. Meaning is constructed and the executive functions are called on as students regularly engage in LCADM. This is not to suggest that there should be no reading or direct instruction. Rather these activities should be meshed with complex problems and projects that personally engage the course content and interests of the learner.

Executive Functions Can Be Sabotaged

Built into the nature of human beings is the possibility for the executive functions to be sabotaged, the result being that the making of meaning can be compromised. The tension is caused by the survival response.

The core point is that when a person experiences fear accompanied by helplessness or fatigue, many higher-order functions are bypassed as the survival response kicks in (Sapolsky, 1998; Peterson, Maier, and Seligman, 1996). This issue too has been examined in many guises, among them the adverse impact of excessive stress (McEwen, 2001; Sapolsky, 1998), the impact of extrinsic rewards and punishments on creativity (Deci and Ryan, 1987; Kohn, 1999), and fear pathways in the brain (LeDoux, 1996).

A detailed account of what happens in the brain has been given by Joseph LeDoux, who distinguishes between what he calls the high road and the low (or survival) road. He offers, by way of example, what happens when a person in the desert comes across what may or may not be a snake. After sensory input occurs, an initial impression of a situation is formed in the amygdala. One response is the high road. That is, higher-order functions in the cortex are invoked as a person thinks and reflects about the situation. This is likely to happen if the person is a naturalist on the lookout for snakes. Another response is the low road. This is an automatic response circuit that leads a person to take immediate action without pausing to think and reflect. It is the basis of fight or flight and is what tends to happen to the uninformed hiker. A significant sense of fear and helplessness trigger the survival response, as a result of which much higher-order cortical activity is likely to be bypassed. Even metabolism slows down (Sapolsky, 1998).

Adult educators can expect a substantial proportion of their students to be (albeit unconsciously) in survival mode. For many adults, taking tests is the equivalent of coming across a threatening snake. For others, speaking or performing in public is the snake. The situation is often exacerbated when a job is at stake and one's everyday existence is contingent on successfully mastering new skills, particularly if the change is rushed and unsupported. If an instructor, however well-meaning, is insensitive to this reality, the student is cast adrift to face the snake alone.

In these circumstances, there is a narrowing of the perceptual field so that, for instance, otherwise obvious cues are missed or misunderstood (Combs, Richards, and Richards, 1988); and reversion to more instinctual or early programmed modes of behavior and less access to higher-order capacities, including metacognitive capacities (LeDoux, 1996).

As might be expected, the survival response also extends along a continuum. Perry (1996) identified five mental states that occur in children but that seem to have analogues for adults. The stages that he identifies are calmness, vigilance, alarm, fear, and terror. The further one moves along the continuum, the more the executive functions are compromised and the more difficult it is to make sense of things and carry out effective decisions (see Perry's Chapter Three in this volume).

All of these reactions play a role in undermining the decisions that learners make as they become more frightened and helpless. In a narrow sense, it becomes difficult for learners to read a situation adequately because the capacity to make sense of things is reduced as relevant information is simply not perceived. In a larger sense, other capacities such as motivation can be adversely affected as fear prevails over interest and optimism. In addition, the ability to take the actions that would ensure further learning is reduced as planning, metacognition, and decision making are compromised. Moreover, each of these responses depends on the stage of developmental maturity of the learner (Kegan, 1994; Taylor, 2006) as well as other factors such as familiarity with a particular context. Thus, the overall process applies universally, but specific responses vary from person to person.

Guides to Action

To begin with, the challenge for both learner and teacher is to initiate and sustain an optimal state of mind for meaningful learning—what we call relaxed alertness (Caine, Caine, McClintic, and Klimek, 2005). This means it is necessary to create conditions that reduce or neutralize the survival response. This is not to say that anxiety and even fear are always inappropriate. They are both natural consequences of confusion, uncertainty, and the need to deal with the problems posed by life. The point is that they should neither be debilitating nor occur inappropriately.

A key to nurturing an appropriate state of mind in learners is the sense of safety and community that is generated in a course or class. Indispensable keys for creating such a community are being listened to and knowing how to listen. This applies to both instructor and students. A useful process that we have employed in many situations is what we call ordered sharing. In essence, students gather in small groups and are given an idea to explore. All persons have the same amount of time to talk, and no one interrupts. In this way, everyone practices listening as people talk, in turn, so that there is no competition for space or time. (For more details, see Caine, Caine, McClintic, and Klimek, 2005, Resource C.) Over time and with practice, people learn to become better listeners, even during active debate and discussion. Instructors also need to master this attitude and skill. One of our solutions is for instructors themselves to meet in small groups (what we call process learning circles) and work with the same procedure among themselves.

In addition to sustaining this state of mind, the learner needs to be immersed in appropriately orchestrated experience, which must be processed and digested both during and after the fact (Caine and Caine, 1994; Schön, 1990). Addressing this fully involves an entire theory and practice of instruction and is beyond the scope of this article. However, here are some preliminary suggestions about how to create conditions that engage the executive brain by encouraging relaxed alertness and reducing the survival response. The solutions suggested here follow in part from research and in part from personal experience in a range of situations, academic and real-world.

Discover and Nourish Purpose and Passion. It is much easier for students to deal with difficult situations and persist with complex problems when the solution or question really matters to them. Within limits (because people who care too much can become dysfunctional), the more they care, the more mental and physical reserves are available to be applied to the learning. Conversely, if learner purposes and interests are disparaged or ignored, or if people are overly invested in a goal or purpose, the survival response can itself be triggered. The pedagogical implication is that what matters to a learner should be connected to curriculum wherever possible, but that the degree of investment that a learner has in the situation and outcomes has to be monitored.

One key is to develop assignments that are driven by student interests. For instance, it is useful to explore why students are taking a particular course and then help them create assignments to connect course content to their own reasons for being there. When students are genuinely interested they are more likely to pay attention, persist longer, and ask relevant questions—if student questions are genuinely welcome and invited.

Learn to Recognize the Survival Mode. It is difficult to cope well when one does not realize that one is feeling threatened or helpless. This reveals itself, for instance, in the person who angrily claims to be calm and in control. Similarly, many educators do not effectively decode students' affective states, particularly when students withdraw inside themselves rather than act out. The path for learners is one of becoming more mature and of developing self-awareness; the path for educators, in addition to focusing on their own growth, is to practice observation and look for clues to what is happening in the body and mind of learners (poker players call these signs "tells").

New Directions for Adult and Continuing Education • DOI: 10.1002/ace

For instance, folded arms and a show of boredom might merely reflect disinterest, but they can also be indicative of self-protection. A student asking questions can be a sign of interest, but a student asking a lot of questions, particularly if they are repetitive, can be a sign of fear and avoidance. Of course, we are not mind readers and so will always be making our own best interpretations. But there are two keys to discerning more accurately what is happening inside a student. The first is to develop a trusting but honest relationship (which takes time, caring, and skill). The second is artful use of questions to elicit clarity without appearing intrusive or overwhelming.

Practice the Art of Scaffolding. One of the classic pitfalls of adult learners is aiming too high and trying to do too much. A proactive approach is for teacher and learner to master the art of scaffolding (Puntambek and Hubscher, 2005). This requires a teacher to help recruit the interest of the learner, develop experiences at an appropriate degree of complexity and difficulty, model and demonstrate and question and process as needed, and allow the scaffolding to fade as a learner becomes competent. Of course, because each person is unique, scaffolding must be adjusted to suit learners and context.

Final Comment

The issues discussed here are directly on the point of adult learning, but they apply in all arenas of life because the processes of making decisions as we make sense of things play out everywhere. The points made in this chapter can be usefully invoked by parents, teachers and coaches, managers and supervisors, and others. All the people with whom one works should engage their executive functions and know how to function and recover when approaching or in survival mode.

References

Bandura, A. "Self-Efficacy: The Foundation of Agency." In W. J. Perrig (ed.), *Control of Human Behavior, Mental Processes, and Consciousness.* Mahwah, N.J.: Erlbaum, 2000.

Bennett, W. J., Finn, E. F., and Cribb, J.T.E. *The Educated Child: A Parent's Guide from Preschool Through Eighth Grade.* New York: Free Press, 2000.

Boone, K. "Neuropsychological Assessment of Executive Functions." In B. Miller and J. Cummings (eds.), *The Human Frontal Lobes: Functions and Disorders.* New York: Guilford Press, 1999.

Caine, G. "Getting It! Creativity, Imagination and Learning." *Independent School,* Winter 2004, pp. 10–18.

Caine, G., and Caine, R. *The Brain, Education and the Competitive Edge.* Lanham, Md.: Scarecrow Press, 2001.

Caine, R., and Caine, G. *Making Connections: Teaching and the Human Brain.* Alexandria, Va.: Association for Supervision and Curriculum Development, 1994.

Caine, R., Caine, G., McClintic, C., and Klimek, K. *12 Brain/Mind Learning Principles in Action: The Field Book for Making Connections, Teaching, and the Human Brain.* Thousand Oaks, Calif.: Corwin Press, 2005.

Collins, A., Brown, J. S., and Holum, A. "Cognitive Apprenticeship: Making Thinking Visible." *American Educator,* 1991, 6–11, 38–46.

Combs, A., Richards, A., and Richards, F. *Perceptual Psychology.* Lanham, Md.: University Press of America, 1988.

Damasio, A. *The Feeling of What Happens: Body and Emotion in the Making of Consciousness.* Orlando: Harcourt Brace, 1999.

Deci, E. L., and Ryan, R. M. "The Support of Autonomy and the Control of Behavior." *Journal of Personality and Social Psychology,* 1987, 53(6), 1024–1037.

Denkla, M. B. "A Theory and Model of Executive Function: A Neuropsychological Perspective." In G. Lyon and N. Krasnegor (eds.), *Attention, Memory, and Executive Function.* Baltimore, Md.: Brookes, 1999.

Goldberg, E. *The Executive Brain: Frontal Lobes and the Civilized Mind.* New York: Oxford University Press, 2001.

Kauchak, D. P., and Eggen, P. D. *Learning and Teaching: Research-Based Methods.* Boston: Allyn & Bacon, 1998.

Kegan, R. *In Over Our Heads: The Mental Demands of Modern Life.* Cambridge, Mass.: Harvard University Press, 1994.

Kohn, A. *Punished by Rewards.* Boston: Houghton Mifflin, 1999.

Lakoff, G., and Johnson, M. *Philosophy in the Flesh: The Embodied Mind and Its Challenge to Western Thought.* New York: Basic Books, 1999.

Lave, J., Wenger, E., Pea, R., Brown, J. S., and Heath, C. *Situated Learning: Legitimate Peripheral Participation.* Cambridge, UK: Cambridge University Press, 1991.

LeDoux, J. *The Emotional Brain.* New York: Simon and Schuster, 1996.

McEwen, B. *The End of Stress as We Know It.* Washington, D.C.: Joseph Henry Press, 2001.

Pennington, B., Vennetto, L., McAleer, O., and Roberts Jr., R. "Executive Functions and Working Memory: Theoretical and Measurement Issues." In G. Lyon and N. Krasnegor (eds.), *Attention, Memory, and Executive Function.* Baltimore, Md.: Brookes, 1999.

Perfect, T. J., and Schwartz, B. L. (eds.). *Applied Metacognition.* Cambridge, UK: Cambridge University Press, 2002.

Perry, B. D. "Neurodevelopmental Adaptations to Violence: How Children Survive the Intragenerational Vortex of Violence." 1996. http://www.childtrauma.org/CTAMATERIALS/vortex_interd.asp; accessed Nov. 12, 2005.

Peterson, C., Maier, S., and Seligman, M. *Learned Helplessness.* New York: Oxford University Press, 1996.

Puntambek, S., and Hubscher, R. "Tools for Scaffolding Students in a Complex Learning Environment: What Have We Gained and What Have We Missed?" *Educational Psychologist,* 2005, 40(1), 1–12.

Sapolsky, R. *Why Zebras Don't Get Ulcers: An Updated Guide to Stress, Stress-Related Diseases, and Coping.* New York: Freeman, 1998.

Schön, D. A. *Educating the Reflective Practitioner: Toward a New Design for Teaching and Learning in the Professions.* San Francisco: Jossey-Bass, 1990.

Schwartz, G. E., and Shapiro, D. (eds.) *Consciousness and Self-Regulation: Advances in Research* (vol. 1). New York: Plenum Press, 1976.

Taylor, K. "Autonomy and Self-Directed Learning: A Developmental Journey." In C. Hoare (ed.), *Handbook of Adult Development and Learning.* New York: Oxford University Press, 2006.

Varella, F. J., Thompson, E., and Rosch, E. *The Embodied Mind: Cognitive Science and Human Experience.* Cambridge, Mass.: MIT Press, 1995.

Zajonc, A. *Catching the Light: What Is Light and How Do We See It?* New York: Oxford University Press, 1993.

GEOFFREY CAINE *is director of the Caine Learning Institute and a process learning coach.*

RENATE NUMMELA CAINE *is executive director of the Caine Learning Institute.*

8 *Social cognitive neuroscience can offer a scientific framework for developmental learning in the mentor-learner relationship.*

The Neuroscience of the Mentor-Learner Relationship

Sandra Johnson

In the mentor-learner relationship, mentors serve as guides in the journey of developmental learning by helping learners become creators of knowledge. Cognitive neuroscience and social cognitive neuroscience provide evidence of changes in the brain resulting from certain aspects of the mentor-learner relationship. Using these scientific frameworks, this chapter examines how mentors promote learners' development by creating trust, being attuned to learners' emotions, and engaging in social interaction that can lead to greater brain plasticity.

Promoting Development Through Trust

Compared with those adult educators who see their work primarily as helping students master course content, mentors believe that learning promotes development and that "development means successively asking broader and deeper questions of the relationship between oneself and the world" (Daloz, 1986, p. 236). According to Brookfield (1987), this happens through "discerning, exploring, and challenging one's own underlying assumptions about the self, society, and reality" (p. 134). A mentor facilitates this journey by inviting learners to question and challenge their assumptions, and by providing emotional support as they do so. Furthermore, during the uncomfortable period of uncertainty and self-questioning, mentors hold out hope by offering a vision of who learners are becoming and of how they will feel when their new sense of self and voice emerges (Daloz, 1999).

NEW DIRECTIONS FOR ADULT AND CONTINUING EDUCATION, no. 110, Summer 2006 © 2006 Wiley Periodicals, Inc.
Published online in Wiley InterScience (www.interscience.wiley.com) • DOI: 10.1002/ace.220

This journey has been described in terms of Perry's landmark research (1968/1999), which identifies learners' transitions from (1) only believing what authorities say, to (2) recognizing that authorities clash and may not always have the answer, to (3) recognizing that each truth has "its own context, meaning, connections that rest on certain assumptions and contain their own inner logic" (Daloz, 1999, p. 75), to (4) shifting into contextual relativism, where "our view of the world is transformed" (p. 75). The first step on this developmental journey with the learner is to "engender trust" (Daloz, 1999, p. 122). By doing so, the mentor builds a nurturing relationship and a "holding environment," which foster development. Winnicott (1965) first used the term *holding environment* to describe how the psychological presence of a caregiver can support a child in beginning to develop her own sense of self.

For adults, according to Daloz (1986), such a holding environment enables us to "consolidate each new sense of self so that we can maintain meaning and coherence in the world and yet remain open to a lifetime of fresh wonders" (p. 190). New technologies that look at the cognitive processes of learning and the neuronal interactions that happen when people interact can now furnish adult educators with scientific understandings of what happens in the brain as a result of the mentor-learner relationship. In short, this new field of educational neuroscience can now demonstrate the vital role of a trusting and safe holding environment in promoting learning and development.

A Neuroscientific Understanding of Trust and Learning

A secure attachment process—one in which trust is established—results in a "cascade of biochemical processes, stimulating and enhancing the growth and connectivity of neural networks throughout the brain" (Schore, 1994, as cited in Cozolino, 2002, p. 191). In other words, caring and encouragement from trusted others promote change in these neuronal networks because the brain is plastic, "in the sense [that] it can be remodeled or physically molded" (Zull, 2002, p. 116). The neuronal networks are also where knowledge is stored; thus, "any change in knowledge must come from some change in neuronal networks" (Zull, 2002, p. 92).

When a mentor is supportive, caring, and encouraging, and offers enthusiasm balanced with an optimal learning environment, learners are assisted in moving their thinking activity into the higher brain regions (the frontal cortex), where reflective activity and abstract thinking take place. (They are called "higher" regions because they are physically above the more primitive parts of the brain that developed earlier in the evolutionary process.) During this process, the learner's neurotransmitters that power the frontal cortex (dopamine, serotonin, and norepinephrine) are stimulated, leading to greater brain plasticity and hence more neuronal networking and meaningful learning (Cozolino, 2002). Experience (learning) changes the

New Directions for Adult and Continuing Education • DOI: 10.1002/ace

wiring (growth and reorganization of neuronal structures) because it changes the activity in the neurons (see also Sheckley and Bell's Chapter Six in this volume).

The discovery that a trusting relationship with a mentor is connected to brain reorganization, growth, and learning underscores what adult educators have long held true: if the mentor creates a safe, trusting relationship and holding environment, learners are much more able to reorganize their thinking and move through the progressive stages of the developmental journey. Two powerful processes that involve the mentor contribute to "both the evolution and sculpting of the brain" (Cozolino, 2002, p. 213): social interaction and affective attunement. These two processes "stimulate the brain to grow, organize and integrate" (Cozolino, 2002, p. 213).

Social Interaction and Affective Attunement

Mentors contribute to the growth and development of learners' brains through social interaction, one form of which is dialogue. Through dialogue, the mentor not only attempts to understand the learner's thoughts, but also raises questions that can stimulate the neuronal process of reflection. While experience is necessary for learning, reflection is *required* because "reflection is searching for connections—literally" (Zull, 2002, p. 164). Thus, dialogue with a trusted other that promotes reflection is a natural way of learning. Our brains search and make neuronal connections between the presented (new) knowledge and what we already know. Reflection, then, is a cognitive process whereby neuronal connections are made; when such connections are made, we have a restructured neuronal map or mental representation of that knowledge. The more neurons there are firing together (that is, the more connections we make while reflecting), the more complex is our neuronal representation of the topic and the longer that neuronal representation will last (Shors and Matzel, 1997).

Social cognitive neuroscience affirms that over eons our brains have developed physical mechanisms that enable us to learn by social interaction. These physical mechanisms have evolved in order for us to be able to acquire the knowledge we need to keep us emotionally and physically safe (Stern, 2004). They enable us to (1) engage in affective attunement or empathic interaction and language, (2) consider the intentions of the other, (3) try to understand what another mind is thinking, and (4) think about how we want to interact (Stern, 2004). These four developmental abilities are the evolutionary underpinnings for reflective social interaction between a mentor and learner.

The notion of affective attunement, another way that a mentor's intervention supports development, harkens back to Dewey's ([1938] 1997) observations that an educator needs to "have that sympathetic understanding of individuals as individuals which gives him an idea of what is actually going on in the minds of those who are learning" (p. 39). According to

New Directions for Adult and Continuing Education • DOI: 10.1002/ace

social cognitive neuroscience, the brain actually needs to seek out an affectively attuned other if it is to learn. Affective attunement alleviates fear, which has been recognized by many in the field of adult learning and development as an impediment to learning (Brookfield, 1987; Daloz, 1986, 1999; Mezirow and Associates, 1991; Perry, [1970] 1998). Our conditioned survival and fear responses come from our primitive brain, also known as the limbic system. We are social beings who look to the tribe for social acceptance; this involves taking on the values and understandings of the tribe. When we begin to question those values—as we do when developing greater cognitive complexity—certain primitive defenses and emotions surface. In effect, when learners start to question authority, they face uncertainty and fear of tribal abandonment (I am not like you and therefore you will reject me).

As learners continue on toward multiplicity, they may feel overwhelmed by varying viewpoints and by "the uncertainty of not being right." This is the time for a dialectical reflective process that can strengthen the connections between the limbic system and the higher areas of the brain: these are called orbitofrontal-limbic connections (Cozolino, 2002). In other words, dialogue between a trusted, affectively attuned mentor and a learner creates the holding environment that assists the learner in moving his or her emotions from the limbic area to the higher regions of the brain (orbitofrontal cortex), where "the voice of reason" is found and the learner can self-modulate those fears. Thus, as we start to see "through the eyes of another" (Daloz, 1986, p. 226) and are able to contextualize new information, we move into abstract thinking. During this process, we also experience pleasure chemicals from the basal structure in the front of the brain that produce a reward that motivates the learner to continue to move along this developmental path.

In writing about the role mentors can play in promoting development, Daloz (1986) understood learners' fears and discussed the need for mentors to "help our students to accept the confusion and uncertainty, to feel safe with it; if we encourage them to enter the darkness to explore those terrifying opposites fully enough, there is a good chance they will begin to move through them on their own and begin to discern a meaning in 'the starless air'" (p. 83).

Creating Spaces of Support

How can adult educators as mentors help learners feel safe enough with confusion and uncertainty to enter into this "darkness"? In other words, how can we assist learners in self-modulating the fears that originate in the limbic system? The key is in the spaces created by the mentor-learner relationship, spaces where the learner feels uniquely seen by the mentor, valued, and safe. This type of relationship creates "a kind of two-person hothouse" (Daloz, 1986, p. 221):

Within its walls, the student can reveal herself in ways that she would not to others for there is an understood quality of trust about it. The relationship becomes a special culture in which certain kinds of growth are encouraged and discouraged. To an extent, the outside world is sealed off, as it must be if this "inside world" is to offer special opportunities not available under ordinary circumstances. Because the experience of being closely listened to is so rare for many people, it can also be just the needed catalyst for the cautious emergence of a new sense of self. By listening, the mentor can give that new self an audience, often for the first time, an ear to hear the first tentative affirmations of a position the student knows to be on her leading edge, ideas too risky to entertain outside the safety of this *space,* a still tender voice speaking itself into being (Daloz, 1986, p. 221).

Social cognitive neuroscience again provides insight into the effects in the brain of what Daloz has called the "space" where the "outside world is sealed off."

Because our first relationships are with our caregivers, cognitive neuroscientists turned to developmental psychology to research the infant-caregiver relationship. They identified profound implications for our future attachment relationships (Stern, 2004). Gallese believes that an infant and caregiver enter an "intersubjective space" (Frith and Wolpert, 2003). This space is created by the infant and caregiver through the process of emotional resonance (Schore, 2002), or affective attunement. It is in this space that the emotional support of the caregiver brings an infant relief from the intense anxiety and fears that originate from the primitive survival mechanisms in the limbic system. The child cannot do this for herself, which is why children are born with evolutionary physical brain mechanisms that enable them to seek out such attachment and receive support. These brain processes continue to develop across our life span because we continually seek out attachment figures with whom we can engage (Stern, 2004).

A particular type of neuron, a mirror neuron, contributes to affective attunement because it enables us to know empathically what another person is feeling (Stern, 2004). When the learner feels her mentor's care and support, her fears start to subside. If she looks into her mentor's eyes and sees reflected what she can become, she will borrow (take in) that confidence until she can produce her own. In other words, mirror neurons will enable her to feel the confidence that her mentor has in her and to join in that confidence.

Although Daloz (1986) discussed being a mirror for the learner—that is, reflecting back her potential—as a metaphor, literally looking into the eyes of the affectively attuned other is another significant form of social interaction that can assist in promoting development. Schore (1994) noted that the orbitofrontal cortex can actually be stimulated through eye contact because specific cells are particularly responsive to facial expression and eye gaze. Caring social signals activate this higher region of the brain and promote learner safety. While this does not explain the phenomenon of effective long-distance mentoring relationships in which eye contact cannot physically be made, it can illuminate how the brain functions when trust and a safe environment are established.

Another specialized space in the mentoring relationship is the zone of proximal development, or ZPD (Vygotsky, 1978). Although this space shares many features with a holding environment (including being safe), the ZPD is where "scaffolding" takes place. Given what we now understand about the relationship between dialogue (questioning and the presentation of new viewpoints) and neuronal triggering, scaffolding can be interpreted in new ways: it can be seen as a process in which the new information is taken in, the learner searches for neuronal connections, and the learner then integrates the old and new knowledge into a reconstructed mental representation. Creativity or abstract thinking is carried out by the brain's executive activity in the integrative front brain (Zull, 2002). The brain reflects and manipulates (or rearranges) the reflected information to create new knowledge or new belief systems. The ZPD can thus be seen as an incubator of abstract thinking or creativity—a place where the power of "a still tender self [can speak] her way into being" (Daloz, 1986, p. 222).

Supporting the Development of Creators of Knowledge

There comes a time in learners' developmental journeys when they are not just receivers of knowledge but creators of it (Zull, 2002). How does a mentor lead a learner into the exhilarating power of her own creative process? Metaphorically speaking, the mentor has a special "radar" or listening device that seeks out the voice of the learner's self. Daloz (1986) believes that "calling the student's voice to emerge is of central importance, for clearly we do not learn to speak unless encouraged to do so, or think without practice" (p. 225).

This type of encouragement from a mentor is vital. Abstract thinking "can be frightening" (Zull, 2002, p. 179): learners are afraid that their ideas may be wrong and that "since these abstract ideas come from the individual brain, they are bound to be different from the ideas of other brains. Abstract ideas may generate conflict. There will be trouble if we all have different ideas" (p. 179). With the emergence of her own voice through the mentor's support, the learner can now take part in a new world—one in which she can contribute through the action of her unique ideas and, best of all, feel the power of her creative spirit, understand the evolvement of that creativity, and perhaps eventually assist another on the evolving journey.

Recent discoveries in cognitive neuroscience and social cognitive neuroscience reveal to educators and mentors of adults the neurological effects and importance of creating a trusting relationship, a holding environment, and an intersubjective space, such as the ZPD, where reflection and abstract thinking can happen. If mentors are to assist learners on the journey from dualistic to multiplistic to contextual thinking, it means choosing to be the guide who "points the way through the fire" (Daloz, 1999, p. 244).

References

Brookfield, S. D. *Developing Critical Thinkers*. San Francisco: Jossey-Bass, 1987.
Cozolino, L. *The Neuroscience of Psychotherapy: Building and Rebuilding the Human Brain*. New York: Norton, 2002.
Daloz, L. *Effective Teaching and Mentoring*. San Francisco: Jossey-Bass, 1986.
Daloz, L. *Mentor: Guiding the Journey of Adult Learners*. San Francisco: Jossey-Bass, 1999.
Dewey, J. *Experience and Education*. New York: Simon and Schuster, 1997. (Originally published 1938.)
Frith, C. and Wolpert, D. *The Neuroscience of Social Interaction: Decoding, Imitating, and Influencing the Actions of Others*. New York: Oxford University Press, 2003.
Mezirow, J., and Associates. *Critical Reflection in Adulthood*. San Francisco: Jossey-Bass, 1991.
Perry, W. G. *Forms of Ethical and Intellectual Development in the College Years*. San Francisco: Jossey-Bass, 1998 (Originally published 1970.).
Schore, A. *Affect Regulation and the Origin of the Self: The Neurobiology of Emotional Development*. Mahwah, N.J.: Erlbaum, 1994.
Schore, A. "Dysregulation of the Right Brain: A Fundamental Mechanism of Traumatic Attachment and the Psychopathogenesis of Posttraumatic Stress Disorder." *Australian and New Zealand Journal of Psychiatry*, 2002, *36*, 9–30.
Shors, T. J., and Matzel, L. D. "Long-Term Potentiation: What's Learning Got to Do with It?" *Behavior and Brain Sciences*, 1997, *20*(4), 597–655.
Stern, D. N. *The Present Moment in Psychotherapy and Everyday Life*. New York: Norton, 2004.
Vygotsky, L. *Mind in Society: The Development of Higher Psychological Processes*. Cambridge, Mass.: Harvard University Press, 1978.
Winnicott, D. W. *The Maturational Processes and the Facilitating Environment*. New York: International University Press, 1965.
Zull, J. E. *The Art of Changing the Brain*. Sterling, Va.: Stylus, 2002.

SANDRA JOHNSON is a mentor for Empire State College, a clinical social worker, and a faculty fellow with the Center for Human Development, Research Foundation of the State University of New York.

9

Recent discoveries about brain function explain how best practices in adult learning may lead to adult learners' developmental growth.

Brain Function and Adult Learning: Implications for Practice

Kathleen Taylor

Our main task in this volume has been to introduce to our colleagues research that we believe holds great promise to support our intentions as adult educators. Since many educators of adults have disciplinary competence in fields far removed from adult learning, let alone neurobiology, we asked our chapter contributors to emphasize issues that would be of particular value to practitioners. This chapter is even more explicit in connecting brain function with adult learning practices chiefly associated with meaningful learning.

As was described earlier in this volume by various authors, what we call mind results from the brain's response to what happens in our body. The brain's essential task is to maintain the organism. It does so by constantly monitoring the body's internal and external state, making adjustments as necessary. The well-known fight-or-flight response, for example, is how the brain tries to ensure survival in the face of a perceived threat. The pleasure response, which involves a different neural pathway, is another method of promoting survival, because it leads the organism toward calorific food, reproduction, and better maternal care of infants. But even when there are no immediate environmental stimuli, the brain monitors and adjusts hormone levels, breathing rate, heart rate, and so on. These responses are located in the most primitive part of the brain, the limbic system, beyond our direct awareness or control.

By contrast, the neocortex and frontal lobes, which have developed more recently but still over many millennia, are considered the civilized parts of the brain (Goldberg, 2001). Through processes I will not attempt to detail

here (see works by Goldberg, Damasio, and Siegel in the References), these two have given rise to what we now call consciousness and associate with mind. Although we still cannot control the release of hormones that signal danger or attraction, we can consciously decide to what extent we will respond to those signals. Even so, the limbic system is at the core of brain function and contributes an image of body state to every memory.

Meaningful Learning

As Pat Wolfe (in Chapter Five of this volume) pointed out, at the synaptic level learning is always about memory, that is, about creating lasting neural connections. But this definition of learning could also apply to stimulus-reward behavioral training, compared with learning that involves self-reflection and creation of meaning. I choose instead to focus on meaningful learning, and particularly on learning that encourages increased cognitive complexity—in other words, learning that changes not just *what* people know but *how* they know. My intention in working with adults is not merely to change observable behavior or add more to their memory bank of experience, but to change how those experiences and memories are stored and retrieved hereafter, because "the most important form of learning involves changing the way a person experiences, conceptualizes, or understands" (Marton, 1992, p. 253).

The changes I wish to emphasize are those that transcend mastering the content of specific courses; they are overarching objectives of adult learning, such as "the understanding that knowledge is neither given nor gotten, but constructed; the ability to take perspective on one's own beliefs; and the realization that learning and development are worthy life-long goals" (Taylor and Marienau, 1997, p. 233). Educators who have such "developmental intentions" (Taylor, Marienau, and Fiddler, 2000) are more likely to enable their learners to understand and respond effectively to what Kegan (1994, 2000) identifies as the demands of modernity. Much of my excitement about and enthusiasm for recent discoveries in brain function stems from the fact that they appear to link best practices in adult learning to the outcomes I have just described.

The major themes in this chapter—constructivism and experiential learning; narrative, autobiography, journals, and writing-to-learn; nonveridical learning; transformational learning and reflection; and the role of emotions and "teaching as care"—are ultimately overlapping and intertwined. The first three, however, concentrate on teaching and learning strategies; the last two are somewhat more focused on theory.

Constructivism and Experiential Learning

Though constructivism was initially a theoretical perspective, the new brain research seems to confirm its basic premise: that learning is constructed in the mind of the learner. (See Caine and Caine, Chapter Seven, in this volume, for some opposing views.) Many external factors may contribute—books, lectures, media, the voices of authorities. There is also always a sociocultural environment that affects how the learning is constructed (Vygotsky, 1978). But even though people may perform functions associated with learning (such as reading and absorbing required data), if those data are not connected to neural networks as meaningful information they are not really learned, in the sense that information is useful for little besides recall. As educators know too well, data that have little meaning to the learner are usually available for recall for only a limited time. Two obvious exceptions are rote learning and mnemonics. Multiplication tables and simple formulae such as the circumference of a circle tend to stick, at least partly because we learned them when we were young—though they may fade if they are not being actively used. Mnemonic devices—such as (E)very (G)ood (B)oy (D)oes (F)ine (the notes written on the treble clef staff)—work because the words that form the phrase or image connect to prior experiences (see Sheckley and Bell's Chapter Six in this volume). In short, given how the brain embodies images, for learning to be both lasting and meaningful it must be experienced (Marton and Booth, 1997).

James Zull's Chapter One in this volume briefly describes the brain architecture that undergirds the four "pillars of learning" he calls gathering, reflecting, creating, and testing. They correspond nicely to David Kolb's learning cycle positions (1984) of concrete experience, reflective observation, abstract conceptualization, and active experimentation. This correspondence looks even more intriguing when one remembers that Kolb adapted and synthesized his model from earlier works by Piaget, Dewey, and Lewin, whose ideas about learning long antedated current understanding of brain function and were based primarily on observation, reflection, and analysis. (Let's hear it for anecdotal evidence filtered through the minds of brilliant observers!)

As Kolb's term *concrete experience* suggests, "a teacher must start with the existing networks of neurons in a learner's brain, because they are the physical form of her prior knowledge" (Zull, 2002, p. 9). Kierkegaard's parallel observation is more philosophical than physiological: "In order to help another [learn] effectively, I must understand what he understands . . . and in the way he understands it" (cited in Kegan, 1994, p 278). Yet many well-meaning instructors introduce new material to adult learners in ways that echo a professional literature review. They start with the Big Picture, situating the material in the broader field in which they are expert, and then narrow to particulars. They point out connections to previous course content as well as look forward to what will follow. Rather than focus on what the learner understands, they focus on what they themselves understand, presuming that is where the learner is also headed. Instructors do this with the best of intentions, that of creating a meaningful context for the learner. But the learner's concrete experience, in such cases, might be merely listening to the *instructor* make meaning.

Although adults may have little or no substantive prior knowledge of a topic, the brain is never a blank slate. Even infants come into the world with previous (admittedly limited) experience. With adults, the situation is reversed. They have a very full slate. Granted, they may not have many relevant neural networks for particle physics or Medieval history. Even so, the brain's approach to processing new data is to search for some experiential connection. If adult learners are not given the opportunity to create such an experience or encouraged to find existing connections that they can build on, they may revert to treating the material as something to be memorized, rather than understood.

Given that the brain embodies experience, doing precedes understanding, particularly in the development of thought (Edelman and Tononi, 2000). (See Sheckley and Bell's Chapter Six.) Because the mind arises from the brain's monitoring of the body, our knowledge of the world is always filtered first through our biological systems and then through our interactions—psychological and social—with the world around us (see Johnson's Chapter Eight in this volume). However, "those interactions do not involve a direct transfer of information" (Edelman and Tononi, 2000, p. 216); we must make meaning before it becomes our own. We are inevitably meaning-making, not meaning-taking, organisms.

On the basis of brain function, a more effective approach than starting with the instructor's Big Picture would be to start with an experience that enables the adult learner to "back into" the new topic rather than meet it head-on. For example, a frontal approach to introducing various adult development theories would probably be for the instructor first briefly to outline the emergence of the study of development within the field of psychology, then to describe major distinctions among various developmental theories, such as age, stage, life task, and so on, associating each with a major theorist.

A more experience-based approach, by contrast, might be to start by asking each adult learner to quickly sketch on a timeline the important personal and professional milestones of his or her life. The class would then be organized in small groups by age and gender, to develop a common narrative, or typical life journey, based on their combined timelines. By facilitating a comparison of these "typical" narratives across groups, an educator could draw out the framework of a developmental progression, underscoring gender and age-cohort differences.

This framework would then inform the assignment to read relevant development theories. Now, however, the course materials become an expansion of learning that these adults already embody, first as people with their own developmental journeys and again when the experience-based activity enables them to reflect on and discover this fact. Rather than adult development being a new and foreign concept, it is recognized as something familiar, of which each of them is a living example. (This and other experiential activities are described more fully in *Developing Adult Learners*, by

Taylor, Marienau, and Fiddler, 2000, which was written before I had read any research on brain function but nevertheless accords with it.)

Although some introductory context for new learning (that is, "advanced organizers") can be helpful, if that context is based almost exclusively on the instructor's knowledge and experience, the pattern-seeking organism that is the brain may not find its own meaningful connection. Most instructors probably (perhaps unconsciously) assume that the learner will make the necessary connections while reading the homework assignment. But after many years of schooling in which learning was equivalent to storing information until the next exam, many adult students approach a reading assignment planning to do exactly that.

By contrast, an experience that creates and anticipates connections between new material and what adults already know—that is, what their mind-bodies have experienced—is much more likely to help them shift from passive to active readers. Metaphorically speaking, their synapses have been primed, so reading becomes more than fulfillment of a required task. This is why, for those of us who *already have* expertise in a particular subject—in other words, lots of existing neural networks based on prior experiences to which we can connect new information—reading a text, listening to a lecture, or simply having a good think can be just as effective as a more "concrete" experience.

Experience-based learning strategies are not limited to introduction of new topics. At any point in the process, learning is enhanced by activities that call on prior or tacit knowledge. (See Sheckley and Bell's Chapter Six.) One group of such activities is based on personal narrative and writing-to-learn.

Narrative, Journals, Autobiography, and Writing-to-Learn

Although these four pedagogical tools can be examined separately from one another, they share the characteristic of being means of learning through articulation. Each is the source of an extensive body of research and literature that will not be reviewed here. Rather, I link these teaching and learning methods to how the brain learns and changes.

Narrative. Some of the most compelling descriptions of the significance of personal narrative as a key to change in the brain come from the field of neuroscience: "The combination of a goal-oriented and linear story-line, with verbal and nonverbal expressions of emotion, activates and utilizes processing of both left and right hemispheres, as well as cortical and subcortical processing. This simultaneous activation may be what is required for wiring and rewiring through the simultaneous or alternating activation of feelings, thoughts, behaviors, and sensations" (Cozolino, 2002, pp. 169–170). However, the benefits of this kind of storytelling, whether oral or written, are not limited to the therapeutic environment.

When adults are given the space and time to describe their experiences with and feelings about a topic, not with the intention of coming up with a right answer but simply to work through their own process of thinking, they are engaging in a version of the narrative procedure Cozolino described. Stephen Brookfield uses a similar approach in what he calls the "critical incident" activity (1990). Students are asked to write details about a particularly challenging professional experience. This is then used in a role-play exercise and as a springboard to ongoing self-examination and peer discussion.

Such coconstruction of narratives with peers and instructor is another important factor in the learning that ensues, because "language and significant social relationships build and shape the brain. . . . Narratives allow us to combine—in conscious memory—our knowledge, sensations, feeling, and behaviors supporting underlying neural network integration" (Cozolino, 2002, p. 292).

Journals. Journals can be considered a specialized subset of the narrative process. From Phyllis Walden's perspective, they help adult learners "develop as knowers . . . [who understand] that knowledge is constructed by the self and others and that truth is contextual" (1995, p. 13). She uses many well-known techniques, including freewriting, list making, Progoff's steppingstones exercise, and one-minute exploration to help adults find and use their individual voice, and also "to capture the present, to reflect on one's life history, and to create the future" (p. 19). This is echoed by Joseph LeDoux's description in *Synaptic Self* of the "distinction between the minimum self and the narrative self. The former is an immediate consciousness of one's self, and the latter is a coherent self-consciousness that extends with past and future stories that we tell about ourselves" (2002, p. 20).

Autobiography. Autobiography is also related to narrative and journaling, with the additional proviso that its primary focus is past experience. In describing how theories of neuroscience and psychotherapy overlap, Lou Cozolino (2002) suggests that "autobiographical memory creates stories of the self capable of supporting affect regulation in the present and the maintenance of homeostatic function into the future"; if adults access such memories, they may "maximize neural network integration" and organization (p. 63).

Engaging in autobiographical narrative can also support a shift in self-awareness associated with development of greater cognitive complexity: "To the extent that our life's experiences contribute to who we are, implicit and explicit memory storage constitute key mechanisms through which the self is formed and maintained. Those aspects of the self that are learned and stored in explicit systems constitute the explicit aspects of the self. To be self-aware is to retrieve from long-term memory our understanding of who we are and place it in the forefront of thought" (LeDoux, 2002, p. 28). Nevertheless, the implicit, hidden parts of the self, which cannot be fore-fronted, continue to affect everything we are and do. Therefore, to the extent that we can make explicit those aspects of our systems of thought that were formerly implicit, we develop more flexible, inclusive ways of knowing. (This is further explored in the later section on transformational learning and reflection.)

New Directions for Adult and Continuing Education • DOI: 10.1002/ace

Prior learning assessment (PLA) is a specialized semiautobiographical process that most educators associate with allowing adults to petition for transcript credit for experiential, extramural learning (Keeton, 1976). Annalee Lamoreaux's thoughtful analysis (2005) of adult learners who associated personal change with the PLA process reveals more substantive outcomes in keeping with the developmental intentions described earlier, including learners' affirmation of learning from experience, consciousness of the role of tacit learning, greater capacity for taking multiple perspectives, and "awareness of consciously creating, modifying, and 'owning' their own perspectives" (p. 76). For example, a learner who, according to Lamoreaux, was coming to see "her experience as object," had this to say: "You're putting it on paper. It's *there,* it's in black and white, you are *reading* your own thought process . . . and when I do that, I [wonder,] 'Is this *really* what I value, is this really what *I'm* thinking, what *I've* learned, what *I* really want to say?' So I look at it, and its *right there*" (original emphasis, p. 107).

Lamoreaux uses a map analogy to describe the progression she identified in these changes. The first position is comparable to discovering that a map can be used to show how one arrived in a particular place; the second is analogous to the discovery that maps can be structured in various ways, depending on the assumptions of the mapmaker; the third, and most sophisticated, is that each of us can be a mapmaker, and the effectiveness of the map depends on the extent to which we recognize our own map-making process.

Writing-to-Learn. Writing-to-learn can be considered a generic form of the narrative process; as described earlier, it is a major tool in self-discovery. As valuable as oral narrative can be, describing and capturing thought in the more precise and concrete form of written prose is a further step in the "process of integration, . . . assessment and recalibration of perception" that may lead to "a set of principles" for future psychological organization (Cozolino, 2002, p. 170). Stories that can be told and (on reflection and analysis) retold "hold the potential for new ways of experiencing ourselves and our lives. In editing our narratives, we change the organization and nature of our memories and, hence, reorganize our brains as well as our minds" (p. 103).

In the absence of such narrative processes, adults may maintain the story of themselves that they internalized at the end of adolescence—a story that is constructed for them by the sociocultural surround (Kegan, 1994). Though it is appropriate at that time of life to take as one's own the rules of adulthood stipulated by one's culture, there are serious limitations to that worldview—limitations that are difficult to discover precisely because *they are* one's worldview. The eye cannot see itself: "How we think about ourselves can have powerful influences on the way we are, and who we become. One's self-image is self-perpetuating" (LeDoux, 2002, p. 320). However, as psychological therapy demonstrates, through the possibility of telling a different story, narrative activities hold the promise of encouraging both a shift in these perceptions and an ongoing "strategy for reediting the self" (Cozolino, 2002, p. 170).

Nonveridical Learning

Most teaching focuses on veridical learning—that is, how to get right answers to problems constructed for that purpose. According to Zull (2002), getting exact answers uses a different part of the brain than decisions that involve comparison, interpretation, and approximation. The former task resides in the front cortex, a major site of language activity. It is most like applying syntax, where the rules are already known. By contrast, examining a problem from multiple perspectives requires reflection, which is centered more in the back cortex. It also takes more time; the brain has to search and sort and then integrate among complex neural pathways. In learning situations that focus intently on coverage, there may be insufficient time to seek new meaning through new constructions of knowledge. But as Gibbs (1992) observed, the teacher's impression of what has been covered is not always matched by the learner's impression.

Veridical learning also draws primarily on the part of the brain most associated with memory, and this tends to look toward the concrete past (see Caine and Caine, Chapter Seven). By contrast, ill-structured problems—those that are open-ended, have many possible solutions, and are far more likely to occur in the real world—require the part of the brain that makes plans, decisions, and choices and creatively looks toward the future (Zull, 2002). Unfortunately, "our whole educational system is based on teaching veridical decision-making. . . . Strategies of actor-centered, adaptive decision making are simply not taught. Instead, they are acquired by each individual idiosyncratically, as a personal cognitive discovery, through trials and errors. Designing ways of explicitly teaching the principles of actor-centered problem solving is among the most worthy challenges for educators" (Goldberg, 2001, p. 83).

Problem-based learning and case studies, when constructed to avoid veridical outcomes, appear to meet Goldberg's worthy challenge. Indeed, many experiential learning activities that include reflection on learning as a process (Taylor, Marienau, and Fiddler, 2000) are likely to invoke adaptive pathways of the brain.

Transformational Learning and Reflection

According to Cozolino (2002), "A basic assumption of both neuroscience and psychotherapy is that optimal health and functioning are related to increasingly advanced levels of growth and integration. On a neurological level, this equates to the integration and communication of neural networks dedicated to emotion, cognition, sensation, and behavior. On a psychological level, integration is the ability to experience important aspects of life while employing a minimum of defensiveness" (p. 26).

New Directions for Adult and Continuing Education • DOI: 10.1002/ace

Mezirow's description of emancipatory or transformational learning strikes a similar note; it can lead to ways of thinking that are increasingly "inclusive, discriminating, and integrative of experience [as well as open] to alternative perspectives" (1991, p. 156). By contrast, people who do not learn or develop such ways of thinking have "rigid and highly defended thought patterns" (p. 156). This suggests that what constitutes optimal health and functioning from the perspective of brain function and psychotherapy is among the goals of adult education. Not incidentally, these are also characteristics of adults who are more epistemologically complex (Kegan, 2000).

Transformational learning practice emphasizes meaning making based on discourse and critical reflection. Such reflective learning depends on discovering and challenging one's own and others' assumptions as a step in establishing new meaning perspectives. These new perspectives can lead to more than just reframes of current ideas; they foster qualitatively more complex ways of understanding and knowing (Kegan, 2000). The frontal lobes, also called the "executive brain," which Goldberg (2001) identifies as the "most uniquely 'human' of all the components of the human brain . . . the 'organ of civilization'" (pp. 23–24), are the most likely seat of this accomplishment.

Such qualitative changes in the form of knowing (epistemology) are "trans-*form*-ative" (Kegan, 2000, p. 49) compared with acquisition of knowledge or modification of behavior. In describing the significance of these changes as outlined in his constructive-developmental model, Kegan (1994) uses an educational metaphor of "contemporary culture as a kind of 'school' and the complex set of tasks and expectations placed upon us in modern life as the 'curriculum' of that school" (p. 3). The developmental task for most adults is to bring to awareness and challenge the premises of beliefs about *how life is* (or *should* be) and *who I am* (or *should* be) that they internalized at the end of psychological adolescence. This is a paradoxical endeavor, however, because it requires examining one's own way of knowing—that is, looking *at* one's lenses of perception, not just *through* them.

Goldberg's description of how the brain might create such new constructs is strikingly similar to Kegan's more psychological description (2000): "the organism must go beyond the mere ability to *form* internal representations . . . [or] models of the world outside. It must acquire the ability to *manipulate* and *transform* these models . . . [that is, to] go beyond the ability to see the world *through* mental [models]; it must acquire the ability to work *with* mental [models]" (original emphasis, Goldberg, 2001, p. 25).

Though often exhilarating, such changes in perspective are not without cost. Questioning the assumptions that have directed one's choices may lead to new and more compelling choices, but many families, communities, and cultures prize continuity over change. The kind of support adults need in order to grow and develop in these ways is discussed further in the section on teaching as care.

Cozolino (2002) suggests that "self-reflective language most likely requires higher levels of neural network integration . . . *Reflexive* language keeps us in the moment, reacting to stressors in the midst of survival. *Reflective* language demonstrates our ability to escape from the present moment, gain perspective on our reflexive actions, and make decisions about what and how we would like to change" (emphasis added, pp. 293–294). In this instance (and somewhat different from common usage), reflexive means reactive, automatic, immediate, not thought through, whereas reflective means the opposite: considered, deliberate, and thoughtful.

This echoes Mezirow's description (1991) of the third form of reflection, critical reflection, which he associates with the potential for transformative learning. The first form of reflection is hypothetical-deductive problem solving, which is the basis for the natural sciences. (In the wake of Hurricane Katrina, one might ask, "What combination of higher levees and restored marshland would limit flood damage in future hurricanes?") The second form of reflection expands beyond the content of a particular problem and its possible solution to the *context* of the problem and one's approach to the solution. This shifts attention from particulars of a specific situation to analysis that has wider application. ("How do we decide, and who decides, what to rebuild following a natural disaster?") However, from a still broader perspective, critical reflection involves questioning the very assumptions or premises that created a particular situation *as* a problem. When, instead of trying to find a solution, attention is turned toward what the question is and why, there is an opening to reflect on and transform "epistemic or psychological presuppositions" (Mezirow, 1991, p. 105). ("How might our view of the relationship between ourselves and the natural environment influence what, where, and whether we decide to rebuild—or build—in the future?")

Veridical learning requires only the first form of reflection Mezirow described. Taking "multiple perspectives" may require the second form of reflection, but if this can be accomplished in an instrumental way—such as by simply citing both sides of a controversy—then it is possible to avoid challenging one's own suppositions. To effectively support critical reflection, learning situations must be constructed that include premise reflection, or "dialectic-presuppositional" logic (Mezirow, 1991). Among the tools that can be a springboard to such reflection are journals, narratives, and other writing-to-learn activities. To encourage transformational learning, however, use of these activities must be "guided by identifying and judging of presuppositions" (Goldberg, 2001, p. 117)—the kind of mental activity that resides in the executive brain.

Reflecting on and questioning presuppositions can bring about changes in how people understand aspects of themselves and their world; such changes become in turn the framework for new beliefs and actions. Vaill (1996) calls this "learning as a way of being" and claims that in today's world of constant challenge and change, which he terms "continuous white water," such sub-

stantive, meaningful, and lasting learning is essential. Indeed, in their longitu-
dinal research on "learning that lasts," Mentkowski and associates (2000)
found that "when learners reflect on deeply held personal beliefs and assumptions, they embrace a transforming developmental challenge, pulling their self-
awareness into an awareness of themselves in a wider world" (p. 202).

The Role of Emotion and Teaching as Care

Emotions are the undercurrent of cognition (Damasio, 1999). As described
earlier, whatever we experience leads the brain to alter our body chemistry;
these changes are the substrate of emotion. In recognizing these emotions,
we discover feelings that tell us what we need to know about the current situation. Hormones can lead us to run away from a bear, or toward a lover.
They can also enhance or retard our capacity to learn. If activated in the way
that is associated with "Aha! What's this? Maybe something interesting?"
(which Caine and Caine in this volume call "quiet attention"), they are
enhancers. The brain is on alert in a positive, receptive way. But if hormones
are pumping because of a perceived or potential threat ("The instructor is
going to call on me and I won't know the answer"), the brain is *less* available for learning. Indeed, "emotions influence our thinking more than
thinking influences our emotion" (Zull, 2002, p. 75).

Long-term memory—that is, circuits made up of durable neuronal patterns—is particularly affected by emotions. Generally, the more powerful the
emotion that accompanies the initial experience, the more lasting the memory. The exception is when the initial experience is so traumatic that dissociation occurs; under these circumstances, memories may be deeply buried
or completely inaccessible to recall (see Perry's Chapter Three in this volume). Memory is the embodiment of emotion tied to experience—not just
"what happened" but "how my body reacted to what happened." Much of
this is implicit memory of which we are not consciously aware, although our
brain is (Gladwell, 2005). This is why a new acquaintance who resembles
someone we loved or despised—that is, who activates neural circuits in the
brain associated with that person—may evoke an instantaneous response of
pleasure or revulsion, even if we do not consciously notice the resemblance.

Unfortunately, "evolution favors anxious genes" (Cozolino, 2002, p.
235). The more fearful and reactive our early forebears were, the more likely
they were to live and reproduce. But in today's less threatening world (at
least in the immediate sense), the tendency toward anxiety can limit our
effectiveness and happiness. (I refer here not to the kind of anxiety that is
diagnosable as a neurosis, but rather the biophysical remnant of our cave-
dwelling ancestor whose life depended on constant alertness to possible
threats.) As described earlier, the more complex kinds of self-awareness—
involving higher brain functions, and with the potential for changes in
neural networks that correspond to changes in our way of knowing—cannot be accomplished when a person feels anxious and defensive. "A *safe and*

empathic relationship establishes an emotional and neurobiological context conducive to the work of neural reorganization. It serves as a buffer and scaffolding within which [an adult] can better tolerate the stress required for neural reorganization" (Cozolino, 2002, original emphasis, p. 291). In other words, adults who would create (or recreate) neural networks associated with development of a more complex epistemology need emotional support for the discomfort that will almost certainly be part of that process (see Johnson's Chapter Eight, this volume).

That said, I would like to revisit a theme introduced in the Editors' Notes: the difference between a therapist and an adult educator. Even as we attend to learners' emotional states, we do not "do therapy." For one thing, it is not our training; but even for those few of us who may have a counseling background, this is not our appropriate professional role as educators. Nevertheless, we cannot escape the fact that many outcomes of approaches to teaching and learning described in this volume are likely to parallel outcomes of professional counseling: greater self-awareness, less anxiety, heightened self-responsibility, increased cognitive complexity. The appropriate role for an educator fostering these outcomes has been described by Daloz in terms of "teaching as care."

Adults who experience education as growthful and changing can nevertheless feel they are standing on the edge of a precipice: "Transformative learning, especially when it involves subjective reframing, is often an intensely threatening emotional experience in which we have to become aware of both the assumptions undergirding our ideas and those supporting our emotional responses to the need to change" (Mezirow, 2000, pp. 6–7). As Brookfield has famously pointed out, learning to question assumptions can, in some communities, lead to "cultural suicide" (1990, p. 153).

Though writing-to-learn, co-construction of narratives (described earlier), and various self-reflective activities can encourage awareness and growth, learning experiences such as these are most effective when they take place within a supportive relationship. Before publication of most of the current literature on brain research, Larry Daloz (1999) used the story of Mentor to describe the kind of relationship that can help another human being along the journey to new ways of perceiving and understanding. There are no simple directions for this kind of attention to and care for another's experience of growth, but Daloz offers memorable and meaningful accounts of his work with adult learners: "When we no longer consider learning to be primarily the acquisition of knowledge, we can no longer view teaching as the bestowal of it. If learning is about growth and growth requires trust, then teaching is about engendering trust, about nurturance—caring for growth. Teaching is thus preeminently an act of care" (Daloz, 1999, p. 237).

This care and nurturance must nevertheless include sufficient challenge. Kegan's description of the "holding environment," the environment on which all development depends, underscores this fact. Kegan (1982) based his notion of the holding environment throughout the lifespan on

Winnicott's observations of infants who, despite the fact that they were fed, clothed, and sheltered, failed to thrive if they were not also held.

According to Kegan, the holding environment comprises three parts: "holding on," "letting go," and "sticking around," or confirmation, contradiction, and continuity. In the learning environment, confirmation affirms the learner by focusing on what he or she has done right, hailing effort, and applauding even small achievements. Contradiction stretches the learner beyond what is comfortable at the moment. Similar to an athletic coach, the educator encourages greater effort, sets high but attainable standards, and helps the adult focus on what remains to be accomplished. Continuity accepts that over time the adult learner's emerging way of being will likely change the structure of the relationship. The power differential shifts as the learner establishes herself as a peer, which invites the educator/mentor to become companion, ally, and colearner (Bloom, 1995). This rarely happens within the confines of a single course, however, and tends to happen more frequently with graduate rather than undergraduate adult learners.

The efficacy of this approach to the mentoring relationship, a balance of support and challenge, is confirmed by the literature on brain function: "We appear to experience optimal development and integration in a context of a balance of nurturance and optimal stress" (Cozolino, 2002, p. 62).

Conclusion

You may have noticed considerable overlap in this chapter's subtopics. For instance, when subject to critical reflection, journaling and autobiography can be ways to construct (and reconstruct) knowledge. Similarly, working with ill-structured problems tends to foster the kind of questioning of premises that leads to transformational shifts in perspective. All of these approaches are most effective when the learner feels supported by a holding environment or mentoring relationship. Furthermore, these teaching and learning strategies can be described in terms of Kolb's learning cycle.

We do not intend to claim, however, that the literature on brain function is the Philosopher's Stone of adult learning. Nor do we imagine that our colleagues in the field of education will become fluent in describing brain architecture (we most certainly are not!). We do, however, hope with this volume to expand the boundaries of the discourse on teaching and learning practices.

In doing so, we realize how important it is to recognize that we adult educators are also engaged in a lifelong process of development and may be experiencing challenges similar to those that we pose for our learners. How do we respond to ideas that call into question our beliefs about our role as educator? How effectively can we bring multiple perspectives to bear on our own practice? Though it has in many ways confirmed my experience, the literature on brain function challenged me to expand beyond my comfort zone. For example, irritated at having to contend with so many unfamiliar anatomical terms, I allowed a thick pile of books to sit on my must-read pile

New Directions for Adult and Continuing Education • DOI: 10.1002/ace

for months, until my responsibilities to a student required action. Even as I resisted and resented the imposition(!), I saw more clearly than ever how many adult learners must feel when their assumptions about their role as learner are called into question.

"The growth and integration of neural networks," Cozolino writes, "is the biological mechanism of all successful learning, including parenting, teaching, and psychotherapy. . . . Challenges that force us to expand our awareness, learn new information, or push beyond assumed limits can all change our brains" (2002, pp. 290–291). More important, however, such new awareness has the potential to change more than the individual's brain: "If you become aware that something *is* in a certain way, then you also become aware that it *could be* in some other way" (original emphasis, Marton and Booth, 1997, p. 207). Adults in whom such awareness develops are likely to be less reactive and more considered in personal, workplace, and political decisions, as well as better able to adapt to changing circumstances. They are also better able to recognize the need for more just, humane, and equitable economic and social structures. In short, they are prone to be more deliberate, responsible, and competent in working toward the health of the commons. For all these reasons, we turn enthusiastically toward research that may support us in encouraging this kind of awareness in our adult learners and ourselves.

References

Bloom, M. "Multiple Roles of the Mentor Supporting Women's Adult Development." In K. Taylor and C. Marienau (eds.), *Learning Environments for Women's Adult Development: Bridges Toward Change.* New Directions in Adult and Continuing Education, no. 65. San Francisco: Jossey-Bass, 1995.

Brookfield, S. D. *The Skillful Teacher.* San Francisco: Jossey-Bass, 1990.

Cozolino, L. *The Neuroscience of Psychotherapy: Building and Rebuilding the Human Brain.* New York: Norton, 2002.

Daloz, L. A. *Mentor: Guiding the Journey of Adult Learners.* San Francisco: Jossey-Bass, 1999.

Damasio, A. *The Feeling of What Happens: Body and Emotion in the Making of Consciousness.* Orlando: Harcourt Brace, 1999.

Edelman, G. M., and Tononi, G. *A Universe of Consciousness.* New York: Basic Books, 2000.

Gibbs, G. *Improving the Quality of Student Learning.* Bristol, UK: Technical and Educational Services, 1992.

Gladwell, M. *Blink: The Power of Thinking Without Thinking.* New York: Little, Brown, 2005.

Goldberg, E. *The Executive Brain: Frontal Lobes and the Civilized Mind.* New York: Oxford University Press, 2001.

Keeton, M. *Experiential Learning.* San Francisco: Jossey-Bass, 1976.

Kegan, R. *The Evolving Self: Problem and Process in Human Development.* Cambridge, Mass.: Harvard University Press, 1982.

Kegan, R. *In Over Our Heads: The Mental Demands of Modern Life.* Cambridge, Mass.: Harvard University Press, 1994.

Kegan, R. "What Form Transforms? A Constructive-Developmental Approach to Trans-

New Directions for Adult and Continuing Education • DOI: 10.1002/ace

formational Learning." In J. Mezirow and Associates (eds.), *Learning as Transformation*. San Francisco: Jossey-Bass, 2000.

Kolb, D. A. *Experiential Learning: Experience as the Source of Learning and Development*. Upper Saddle River, N.J.: Prentice Hall, 1984.

Lamoreaux, A. "Adult Learners' Experience of Change Related to Prior Learning Assessment." Unpublished dissertation, Walden University, 2005.

LeDoux, J. *The Synaptic Self: How Our Brains Become Who We Are*. New York: Penguin Books, 2002.

Marton, F. "Phenomenography and 'the Art of Teaching All Things to All Men.'" *Qualitative Studies in Education*, 1992, 5(3), 253–267.

Marton, F., and Booth, S. *Learning and Awareness*. Mahwah, N.J.: Erlbaum, 1997.

Mentkowski, M., and Associates. *Learning That Lasts: Integrating Learning, Development, and Performance in College and Beyond*. San Francisco: Jossey-Bass, 2000.

Mezirow, J. *Transformative Dimensions of Adult Learning*. San Francisco: Jossey-Bass, 1991.

Mezirow, J., and Associates. *Learning as Transformation*. San Francisco: Jossey-Bass, 2000.

Siegel, D. J. *The Developing Mind*. New York: Guilford Press, 1999.

Taylor, K., and Marienau, C. "Constructive-Development Theory as a Framework for Assessment in Higher Education." *Assessment and Evaluation in Higher Education*, 1997, 22(2), 233–243.

Taylor, K., Marienau, C., and Fiddler, M. *Developing Adult Learners: Strategies for Teachers and Trainers*. San Francisco: Jossey-Bass, 2000.

Vaill, P. *Learning as a Way of Being*. San Francisco: Jossey-Bass, 1996.

Vygotsky, L. *Mind in Society: The Development of Higher Psychological Processes*. Cambridge, Mass.: Harvard University Press, 1978.

Walden, P. "Journal Writing: A Tool for Women Developing as Knowers." In K. Taylor and C. Marienau (eds.), *Learning Environments for Women's Adult Development: Bridges Toward Change*. New Directions in Adult and Continuing Education, no. 65. San Francisco, Jossey-Bass, 1995.

Zull, J. E. *The Art of Changing the Brain*. Sterling, Va.: Stylus, 2002.

KATHLEEN TAYLOR *is a professor in the school of education at Saint Mary's College of California.*

INDEX

Actor-centered adaptive decision making (ACADM), 55–56

Adult educators: brain research and, 3, 8, 11; as caring mentors, 14–15, 82; hemispheric balance and, 15; holding environment and, 83; as suppliers of new experiences, 8; traumatized learners and, 25. *See also* Mentors

Adult learners: negative assumptions of, 14–15; learning traumas of, 14, 16, 25; self-esteem of, 16; survival responses of, 24–25. *See also* Narratives, learner; Traumatized learners

Adult learning: anger and, 14–15; cognitive neuroscience and, 3, 8, 11; concept mapping and, 49; fear and, 14, 25; over lifespan, 11; new experiences and, 8, 37; peer-learning strategy in, 17; response to threat and, 24; social-emotional environment and, 13; storytelling and, 17; stress and, 13–14. *See also* Adult educators; Adult learning, practice implications for; Learning

Adult learning, practice implications for: advanced organizers and, 75; autobiographies and, 76–77; Big Picture approach and, 74; critical incident activity and, 76; experience-based strategies and, 74–75; frontal approach and, 74; journals and, 76; meaning construction and, 73; meaningful learning and, 72; narratives and, 74–76; nonveridical learning and, 78; timelines and, 74; writing-to-learn and, 77–78. *See also* Instructional strategies, for meaningful learning

Affective attunement, 66

Analogy, learning and, 38

Anger, and learning, 14

Arousal: learning and, 12–14; memory and, 39; stress response and, 13–14, 23, 39

Arousal continuum, 23–24

Associations, neocortex and, 4, 6

Attention, and learning: definition of, 36; emotion and, 39–40; habituation and, 37; meaning and, 36–39; novel events and, 37; psychopysiology of, 36–37

Autobiographies: prior learning assessment and, 77; self-awareness and, 76. *See also* Journals

Avoidance, 24

Baseline, of fear state, 25

Bell, S., "Experience, Consciousness, and Learning: Implications for Instruction," 43–51

Biological reductionism, 30

Biopsychosocial model, of mental illness, 30

Brain: amygdala, 39; bauplan of, 3–4; change-of-body-state (COBS) experience and, 43–44; cortex, 3; as dynamic, 36; fired-together-wired-together (FTWT) networks in, 36, 43–49; hippocampus and, 31; limbic system, 15, 66; mind and, 30–31; neocortex, 3–4; orbitofrontal cortex and, 15, 79; as pattern-making organ, 37; response to threat and, 22–24; signaling and, 3; as social organ, 13, 15. *See also* Brain, change in; Executive functions, of brain; Neocortex

Brain, changes in: affective attunement and, 66; challenges and, 84; emotion-induced, 39; fear-induced, 24–25; and learning, 4–5, 7, 11, 22; mental illness and, 30; by mind, 30; narratives and, 75; neural plasticity, 11–112, 14; psychological trauma and, 30; reflection and, 32; safe space and, 67; social interaction and, 65; stress-induced, 22; transformational learning and, 79; in traumatized learners, 22–24; trauma-induced, 22; trust and, 64–65. *See also* Brain self-repair

Brain development: brain plasticity and, 32; education and, 31–32; genes and, 32; learning and, 32; psychological trauma and, 32; reflection and, 32; research on, 33; safe space and, 67

"Brain Function and Adult Learning: Implications for Practice," 71–85

Brain plasticity. *See* Neural plasticity

Brain self-repair: education and, 31–32; hippocampus and, 31; mind and, 30;

24–25; baseline state and, 25; classroom experiences and, 14–15; curiosity and, 26–27; information retrieval and, 26; long-term impact and, 25–26
"Fear and Learning: Trauma-Related Factors in the Adult Education Process," 21–28
Fight-or-flight response, 22–24, 39. *See also* Stress response
Fired-together-wired-together (FTWT) networks, 36, 43–49

Habituation, 37
Holding environment, 82–83. *See also* Safety, and learning
Hypothetical-deductive problem solving, 80

Information retrieval, fear and, 26
Instructional strategies, and consciousness: concept mapping and, 49; conceptual models and, 48; linking to new ideas as, 48; real-life experiences and, 49–50, 74; reflection and, 47; strategy 1: begin with baseline of prior experience, 46–47; strategy 2: extend learners' consciousness, 47–49; strategy 3: enrich consciousness, 49–50; tacit knowledge and, 49–50
Instructional strategies, for meaningful learning: actor-centered adaptive decision making, 55–56; cognitive coaching, 54; concept mapping, 49; creating safe environment and, 58–59; listening, 58–59; nourishing purpose/passion and, 59; orchestrating experiences for, 59; ordered sharing, 59; recognizing survival mode and, 59–60; scaffolding, 60; situated cognition, 54

Johnson, S., "The Neuroscience of the Mentor-Learner Relationship," 63–69
Journals, 76. *See also* Autobiographies

"Key Aspects of How the Brain Learns," 3–9
Knowledge creation, learner development and, 68
Kolb's learning cycle, 5

Learner transitions, 64. *See* Developmental journey, of learner

Learners. *See* Developmental journey, of learner; Narratives, learner
Learning: activation of affective-cognitive processes and, 13; arousal and 12–14, 26; aspects of, 53; brain changes and, 4–5, 7, 11; brain development and, 32; as change, 4; constructivist view of, 7; decision making and, 55; four pillars of, 5–7, 73; Kolb's learning cycle and, 5, 73; making of meaning and, 53–55; neural basis of, 33–37; neural plasticity and, 11–12; neurobiological factors in, 4–5, 7, 14; neurophysiology of, 1, 3, 8, 11, 13; NSF-funded research on, 33; plasticity and, 13; principles for enhancing, 12; problem solving and, 38; project-based, 38–39; psychosociological theories and, 1; self-reflection and, 13; top-down convergence and, 15; veridical vs. nonveridical, 78; window for, 7–8. *See also* Adult learning; Experiential learning; Instructional strategies *(by specific topic)*; Meaningful learning; Narratives, learner; *and by specific topic*; Transformational learning
Learning theory: behavioral measures, 35; cognitive structuring/restructuring, 35; constructivism, 38, 53–54
Limbic system, 15
Long-term memory, 81

Meaning, and learning: attention and, 36–39; concrete experience and, 38, 74; embodied meaning and, 54; metaphor/analogy/simile and, 38; misconceptions and, 37; prior knowledge and, 38; problem-solving and, 38–39; projects and, 39; retention and, 36; visualization and, 37. *See also* Meaning making
Meaning making: actor-centered adaptive decision making (ACADM) and, 55–56; cognitive coaching and, 54; constructivism and, 53–54; embodied meaning and, 54; experience and, 54–55; individual nature of, 54; learning and, 53; perception and, 54; situated cognition and, 54; sociocultural context and, 73
Meaningful learning: constructivism and, 53–55; creating environment for, 58–59; definition of, 53; practice

**NEW DIRECTIONS FOR
ADULT AND CONTINUING EDUCATION
IS NOW AVAILABLE ONLINE AT WILEY INTERSCIENCE**

What is Wiley InterScience?

Wiley InterScience is the dynamic online content service from John Wiley &
Sons delivering the full text of over 300 leading scientific, technical, medical,
and professional journals, plus major reference works, the acclaimed *Current
Protocols* laboratory manuals, and even the full text of select Wiley print books
online.

What are some special features of Wiley InterScience?

Wiley InterScience Alerts is a service that delivers table of contents via e-mail
for any journal available on Wiley InterScience as soon as a new issue is
published online.
Early View is Wiley's exclusive service presenting individual articles online as
soon as they are ready, even before the release of the compiled print issue.
These articles are complete, peer-reviewed, and citable.
CrossRef is the innovative multi-publisher reference linking system enabling
readers to move seamlessly from a reference in a journal article to the cited
publication, typically located on a different server and published by a different
publisher.

How can I access Wiley InterScience?

Visit http://www.interscience.wiley.com

Guest Users can browse Wiley InterScience for unrestricted access to journal
Tables of Contents and Article Abstracts, or use the powerful search engine.
Registered Users are provided with a *Personal Home Page* to store and
manage customized alerts, searches, and links to favorite journals and articles.
Additionally, Registered Users can view free Online Sample Issues and preview
selected material from major reference works.
Licensed Customers are entitled to access full-text journal articles in PDF, with
select journals also offering full-text HTML.

How do I become an Authorized User?

Authorized Users are individuals authorized by a paying Customer to have
access to the journals in Wiley InterScience. For example, a university that
subscribes to Wiley journals is considered to be the Customer. Faculty, staff and
students authorized by the university to have access to those journals in Wiley
InterScience are Authorized Users. Users should contact their Library for information on which Wiley journals they have access to in Wiley InterScience.

ASK YOUR INSTITUTION ABOUT WILEY INTERSCIENCE TODAY!

Printed in the United States
136310LV00005B/7/A